Great
Racing Drivers

Great
Racing Drivers
Doug Nye

Hamlyn
London · New York · Sydney · Toronto

Acknowledgements

The publishers are grateful to the following individuals and organisations for the illustrations in this book: Associated Press; *Autocar*; Maxwell Boyd; British Petroleum; Diana Burnett; D.P.P.I.; Geoffrey Goddard; Gulf; David Hodges; Indianapolis Motor Speedway;Keystone Press Agency; London Art Tech; Don Morley/All Sport; *Motor*; *Motor Cycle*; Phipps Photographic; Cyril Posthumus; Stanley Rosenthal; Shell; Nigel Snowdon; David Stone; Gerry Stream; Robert A. Tronolone; Yardley; Bob Young.

Published by The Hamlyn Publishing Group Limited
London · New York · Sydney · Toronto
Astronaut House, Feltham, Middlesex, England
Copyright © The Hamlyn Publishing Group Limited 1977

ISBN 0 600 37569 2

Filmset in Great Britain by Tradespools Limited, Frome, Somerset
Printed in Italy by New Interlitho Limited, Milan

Contents

Introduction

The popular public impression of the racing driver is coloured largely by comic-cuts race reporting or gossip-writing in the mass media. Their picture of a jut-chinned, blue-eyed dare-devil, shrugging off a bevy of beautiful girls just in time to stride to his car, smash the loud pedal to the floor and bullet fearlessly away at record-shattering pace is generally accepted.

But this impression of a mindless hero 'laughing gaily in the face of death' makes no concession to the intrinsic dedication and skill which combine to form the genuine, real-life, great racing driver.

Our champion drivers appear in all shapes and sizes, and although their current girth is strictly limited by the capacity of modern single-seater cockpits we still have short stocky ones, tall thin ones, and every possible combination of the two. Many of the very fastest are far from being jut-chinned and blue-eyed, although with very rare exceptions their eyes are particularly bright, beady and penetrating.

Good eyes are a basic requirement for the genuine ace. Broad shoulders and brawny arms have also become standard equipment, for however proud he might be of his lower regions all the racing driver's power is in the upper half of his body. Today's drivers, reclining in cars with enormous cornering power, also develop immensely strong neck muscles to support their helmeted heads against pitiless 'g' forces.

To some extent the media's idea that all racing drivers are fearless is true. Some lack the brain power to recognise fear when they experience it, others can be physically sick from pre-race tension yet perform like Superman once the flag has dropped. Fear comes from the unknown and these men know full well what they are doing, and have subconsciously assessed every situation they are likely to encounter. For most of his track time the racing driver has to work far out on the extreme limits of his own ability, and the essence of competition is that there can be little held in reserve.

It is the degree of reserve which can make a great racing driver as opposed to 'just' a good one, for the Greats of motor racing history have been those men who could hold off the opposition with skill to spare. Only when an unexpected factor suddenly introduced itself into the performance equation would this reserve of skill flash into blinding action. Very, very few people can have been on the spot to see those frantic moments when the really great drivers such as Nuvolari, Fangio, Moss, Clark or Stewart had to draw on their reserves, and so salvaged a situation which could have spelt disaster to a less extraordinary mortal.

I use that term in a relative sense, for the experience of being driven around any racing circuit by even a consistent Grand Prix back marker of the 1960s is very impressive. One's reaction might be, 'My God I could never do that — I'm not brave enough', and it gives some idea of just how hard the real aces must press on when the chips are down. Ride with them and the re-action would be hard to put into words. While one might not be brave enough to do what the back-marker did with his car, the performance of the true ace is on an unreal level — 'Even if I was brave enough there is no way I could make a car do *that*!' might sum it up. While the experienced also-ran — by which I mean all but the supreme two or three at any given time — would be catching and controlling every incipient slide, lurch and twitch of his car, the true ace would be operating ahead of his machinery. He would be *making* it slide, lurch and twitch as he required, and every single movement of that living machine in which he sat would be funnelled into achieving his target of the shortest attainable time on every vital lap. Add the complication of close competition, when the name of the game becomes staying in front as the primary aim, and quick lap times become a mere by-product, and motor racing becomes a truly combative activity.

Perhaps it is luck which gives the truly great racing drivers the natural attributes which make them great. While they do not need to be as well-muscled as a boxer, pole-vaulter or hurdler they have to be very nearly as fit and their perceptive abilities have to be exceptional. Their keen eyes and supremely-sensitive balance organs must feed the brain with stimuli upon which its nerve systems can react with nano-second reflex, sparking sinew and muscle into those finely-judged actions which balance a car on that slippery knife-edge between optimum performance and calamity.

Such basic equipment must be inborn, while conditioned reflexes can be learned by long and hard experience, by time spent in the rarefied environment of a racing car at speed. Experience has made winners out of drivers with relatively little going for them naturally, but who have compensated with all the determination and dedication in the world. Some of these drivers are included in our list of 'greats' but they have never become the standard-setters of their time — they are not the equal of Nuvolari, Fangio, Moss, Clark and Stewart.

Determination and dedication are the two vital psychological ingredients in the great racing driver's make-up, or indeed in any kind of genuine Competitor with a capital 'C'. The will to prove oneself *best* is a naturally male instinct. In some it is better-developed, or has lingered more fully from our days in the trees, than in others and these are the high-attainment individuals to whom second place simply is not good enough.

These are the people who become the ace tennis players, big money winning golfers, high-stakes gamblers or Champion racing drivers. Often their psychology makes them far from the most likable people one could meet, but among all these competitive characters the stars of motor racing are unique.

There are many aspects to their sport — and in recent years the ability to test, develop and tailor their cars to their own personal requirements has become as important as sheer speed in qualifying and intelligent pace in the race itself. The men who combine these talents best with a competitive car are those who win races, regularly.

Their sport is not a game played on a proscribed pitch or court. Every circuit on which they race is different (despite near-standardisation in recent years). Racing drivers have to contend with the naturally fickle nature of highly-tuned machinery, and their environment is such that a bad mistake, a mechanical failure — or perhaps more alarmingly those of a fellow competitor — could cost much more than a simple loss of time or points. Violent bodily harm and perhaps death are an ever present penalty for getting it wrong. Motor racing at its highest level is a game played for keeps, and to many this is a total attraction.

Once in his car the racing driver is perfectly alone. Nobody can help him, coach him or encourage him out there on circuit. He has a signal link with his pit crew once a lap. Occasionally radio links have been used but they usually prove too distracting. For long minutes the racing driver must work at a fully-extended level of speed and concentration, perception and instant action never experienced by 99·99 per cent of his species.

This is a sportsman of the 20th century; at the same time master of his own destiny yet a slave to his competitive instinct. He is the Great Racing Driver . . .

The Early Drivers

Just like the motor car itself, the profession of 'racing driver' was not invented — it simply evolved. In the beginning anyone who drove or entered his horseless carriage in a motor race became known as a 'racing motorist', and as driving in motor races became an honourable activity so the 'racing driver' came into being.

Until that time it had probably been as offensive to call somebody a 'driver' as it would be today to call them a 'peasant', for the term smacked of servitude. It took the heroic events of the great era of City-to-City races to dispel that inference, for in those races qualities of skill, stamina and very real courage were demonstrated for all to see. 'The racing driver' quickly became a celebrity. The really great drivers became national heroes . . .

Although a steamer race was held in Wisconsin, USA, as early as 1878, there are firm grounds to say that, organised motor sport was born in France, only two years after Carl Benz had produced his first practicable automobile in Germany. It was 1887, and M. Fossier, editor of the French journal *La Vélocipede,* arranged a run along the banks of the River Seine in Paris, from St James to Neuilly. Unfortunately only one runner turned-out for the event, Georges Bouton on a steam-powered quadricycle, but he completed the run without mishap.

In 1888 Fossier tried again, and a race of sorts from Neuilly to Versailles again fell to Bouton, whose De Dion tricycle proved faster than a Serpollet steam car.

We had to wait until 1894 to see a well-supported motor competition with mass entries from petrol-engined cars. This was the Paris—Rouen Trial — not a race — organised by the newspaper *Le Petit Journal*

It was a great success, and some of its entrants and organisers formed themselves into a Committee which was in turn to evolve into the Automobile Club de France. For 1895 they organised the first true motor race, and they laid their plans on a grand scale which gave automobile design and development a terrific incentive for improvement.

Although the motor car was only ten years old at that time, and the roads of the day were largely unsealed, became quagmires in rain and threw up choking clouds of dust when dry, they chose a monster course from Paris to Bordeaux and back, over a distance of 732 miles!

Emile Levassor drove without relief in his Panhard — 'Old No 5' as it was to become known — to cover the route in 48 hr 48 min at an average of 15·25 mph. This remarkable feat of stamina and endurance has barely been equalled since, and today a vast and heroic monument 'Á Levassor' stands near the scene of that race's finishing line at the Porte Maillot, in Paris.

It commemorates the first great racing driver, but in fact Levassor's Panhard was proscribed by the race regulations, being a two-seater, and first prize for the Paris—Bordeaux went to Koechlin's Peugeot, which clattered home 11 hours later. There is no memorial to Koechlin, and even his christian name seems to have passed unrecorded . . .

Only six other petrol-engined cars and one steamer survived this gruelling motor racing baptism, but it had proved a huge success and established the mainstream framework of European motor sport for the succeeding six years. This was the heroic age of City-to-City events, which were much more akin to modern rallies than to modern racing.

Experience with the Paris—Bordeaux persuaded the organising Club to institute overnight stops, time controls and neutralised sections in future major events, for a feat of endurance such as Levassor's could well prove fatal to a lesser man on a faster car, or to a driver with less resistance to fatigue.

So the late 1890s saw the high-built, spindly-wheeled, short wheelbase vehicles of the time rushing about the countryside from point to point; normally with a driver and riding mechanic seated high, terribly exposed to the elements, and often carrying passengers, along 'just for the ride'.

As speeds increased with the forced pace of technical development, so the riding crews began to adopt protective clothing, with thick furs, leather or macintosh coats, strap-on helmets, goggles and often sinister-looking leather face masks. Dust and flying pebbles which could prove a nuisance at 25 mph in 1895 had become blinding potential killers for crews racing at 50—60 mph in 1899.

This age of City-to-City racing crunched to a sickening halt on May 24, 1903, when the Paris—Madrid race was forcibly halted at Bordeaux following a string of fatal accidents, many involving the carefree spectators who swamped the route. Fernand Gabriel, who was declared winner of the race, had *averaged* 65·3 mph in his Mors for the 342 miles to Bordeaux, while Louis Renault's 30 hp light car was said to have averaged nearly *ninety* miles per hour from Bonneval to Chartres.

This is a startling measure of the progress made in those early days, and the racing car had already emerged as a distinctly separate identity, totally different to the production models of the time.

Before the calamities of the Paris—Madrid brought this era to a halt, much of the manufacturers' energy had been diverted by the first international race series. This had been inaugurated by the proprietor of the *New York Herald*

newspaper, James Gordon Bennett, and was intended to compare the best three-car teams the manufacturing nations could produce. The series ran from 1900 to 1905, by which time the French — who had the largest motor industry in the World — lost patience with the equality given to lesser nations by the Gordon Bennett rules. They refused to organise another race for his Trophy, and introduced their own *Grand Prix* in its place.

The first *Grand Prix de l'Automobile Club de France* was run on the 64-mile Sarthe circuit outside Le Mans on June 26—27, 1906, six laps of the course having to be covered on both days. Eleven of the 32 starters reached the finish, and the Hungarian Renault works tester, Ferenc Szisz, won at 62·88 mph in one of his company's cars.

Szisz was a typical driver of his time, a solid, reliable works mechanic turned racing ace. He had come to France in 1900, at the age of 27, and had joined the Renault Freres factory at Billancourt. He served as riding mechanic to Louis Renault, before becoming chief tester and failing to qualify for the 1905 French Gordon Bennett team. Later that season he ran second in the American Vanderbilt Cup race on Long Island, and then came his terrific triumph in the classic Grand Prix.

He never achieved such success again, and he went into virtual retirement from 1908—14 when he reappeared in the Grand Prix at Lyon in an Alda. He was forced to retire from the race when he was struck by a passing Opel while changing tyres by the roadside, but his injuries were minor, and eighteen days later he won the Circuit of Anjou race at Rochefort in his kind of car — a monster 12-litre Lorraine-Dietrich.

The winner of the first Grand Prix never raced again, and this quiet, unassuming and practical little man lived until he was 97, dying in the Hungarian village of Tiszaszentimre as recently as 1970!

This race established the mainstream of European motor racing which has survived and flourished to this day. Circuit racing itself was not new,

Champion of France — Georges Boillot during his 965-mile two-day drive to win the 1912 Grand Prix de l'ACF at Dieppe. His 7·6-litre Peugeot set a trend for four-valve per cylinder twin-overhead camshaft racing engines — despite its evident thirst for oil

for as early as May 1, 1898, the 90-mile, one-lap *Course de Perigueux* had been run on a closed loop of roads. Unfortunately the event was marred by the first immediately fatal racing accident, in which the Marquis de Montaignac's heavy tiller-steered Landry et Beyroux collided with De Montariol's Benz *Parisienne* a mile from the start. Both vehicles overturned, and of the four crewmen involved two died (including the hapless Marquis) and a third was critically injured.

In 1900 the *Course du Catalogue*, run over two laps of a 45-mile circuit near Melun, gave a preview of things to come, and one week later the more important circuit meeting of the *Course du Sud-Ouest* was run outside Pau. On July 31, 1902 a really major event was fought out for the first time on a closed circuit; this was the *Circuit des Ardennes*, run over six laps of the 53-mile Bastogne course — centred on the town later to become bloodily famous in the winter of 1944–45.

In the years before the First World War, Grand Prix racing flourished until 1908, when the hated Germans won the race at Dieppe, and then there was a three-year hiatus as the French

industry suffered a recession and concentrated upon light car 'Voiturette' racing. In 1912–13 the Grand Prix was revived, and Georges Boillot won it for Peugeot in both years to establish himself as a national hero.

While Levassor, Girardot, the Chevalier de Knyff, Charron, the Renault, Fournier and Farman brothers and Leon Théry had proved themselves the great names of the City-to-City and Gordon Bennett era, Georges Boillot was the first brilliant star of Grand Prix racing.

He was a flamboyant, luxuriously moustachioed, expansive Frenchman, with a superb theatrical sense. Born in 1885 he had raced the peculiar long-stroke Lion-Peugeots from 1908, and his extrovert driving took the 7·6-litre Peugeot to victory from Wagner's monstrous old-style chain-driven FIAT in the 1912 Grand Prix at Dieppe. He won for a second time at Amiens, in 1913, and was the sentimental star — the passion — of the tremendous 1914 Grand Prix, held on the 23-mile Lyon-Givors circuit.

There, Boillot made full use of his new Peugeot's four-wheel brakes to fight a phalanx of white Mercedes cars from Germany, but the Peugeot handled indifferently through the corners and inexorable pressure from the Mercedes slowly wore down both Boillot and his car. With less than 40 miles to run the blue Peugeot died out on the circuit, and while Boillot accepted the frustration of this his last race, the German cars finished 1–2–3 to a stony reception.

Boillot joined the forces as Europe plunged into war, first as a chauffeur and then as a pilot. It suited both his natural skill and, perhaps, his unrivalled talent as a *poseur*. On May 21, 1916, the much-loved Champion of France plunged to his death on the pock-marked battlefield of Verdun.

If Georges Boillot exemplified rumbustious skill and daring in this period then his tormentor at Lyon, Christian Lautenschlager, was his complete antithesis.

Lautenschlager was a simple Swabian working man made good. He was foreman of Daimler's inspection and running-in department, and had ridden as mechanic on Mercedes racing cars as early as 1906. His first race as driver was the 1908 Grand Prix at Dieppe, and he won it when Victor Hémery — leading in a Benz — suffered an eye injury and was forced to slow down. Thereafter the stolid Swabian artisan stayed happily in Daimler's test shop, until 1913 when he finished sixth on the company's return to racing in the minor *Grand Prix de France* at Le Mans. In 1914 it was his impassive, inexorable speed which wore down Boillot's Peugeot and so he won the greatest Grand Prix of all. Lautenschlager drove for Mercedes again after the war, including the Indianapolis 500 among his races, but success was beyond him, and he retired after the 1924 season, aged 47. He stayed with his life-long employer until his death in the spring of 1954.

The Italian, Felice Nazzaro, was another great ace of these early years,

and while he had the inborn natural talent of Boillot he applied it with the cool precision of a Lautenschlager. His driving looked smooth and unflurried. Any impression of speed was almost disguised by his coldly-calculated mechanical sympathy, but the watches told a different story — he was one of the fastest of them all.

Nazzaro had been apprenticed to the Ceirano company at 15, and when they merged into FIAT in 1899 he was working with Vincenzo Lancia in the test department. Both started racing FIAT cars in 1900, and in the following year Nazzaro won the *Giro d'Italia*. He became chauffeur to Count Florio — founder of the Targa and Coppa Florio races — and 1907 was his year. He won all three major events; the Targa Florio, the Grand Prix and the Kaiserpreis, and many aspiring drivers began to model themselves on the unflurried, smooth style of 'The Great Nazzaro'.

Victory — weary but still immaculate in shirt and tie, Felice Nazzaro is chaired from his car after winning the 1922 French Grand Prix at Strasbourg. It would appear he had yet to be told of his nephew Biaggio's fatal accident

This un-Italian Italian's fortunes dulled before the First World War, although he built his own cars and won the 1913 Targa Florio in one of them. After the war he returned to Fiat and at the age of 41 won them the 1922 French Grand Prix at Strasbourg. He was second in the Italian Grand Prix and remained with Fiat as a deeply respected staff member until his death at the early age of 59 in 1940.

Meanwhile, track racing had begun on Britain's Brooklands Motor Course as early as 1907, and was later developed in America at Indianapolis and on the board tracks. One great driver who excelled equally on road and track was the Italian-born, London-domiciled Dario Resta.

He had come to England with his parents in 1886, aged two, and grew up as an Englishman. He opened his own garage and made his racing debut in the opening Brooklands meeting, driving a client's Mercedes. By 1912 he was in the Sunbeam team, and shone in the Coupe de l'Auto for Voiturette cars run concurrently with the revived Grand Prix. He placed second in the Coupe after leading it until the last lap, and was fourth overall in the Grand Prix.

Resta shone in record-breaking and in 1914 he left for America on business and was talked into driving a Peugeot for the importers there. He achieved staggering success, and by 1916 he was capable of winning Indianapolis and the National Championship — the only foreigner ever to do both.

After the war, Resta returned to Sunbeam and raced and won for them until the end of 1924 when he attacked some records at Brooklands, where his glittering career had begun 17 years previously. At 120 mph a security bolt suddenly broke and punctured a tyre. The Sunbeam clattered through iron fencing beside the Railway Straight and Resta was killed and his mechanic, Perkins, seriously injured. This truly great racing driver was mourned equally on both sides of the Atlantic.

In the early 1920s more national Grand Prix races were established, following France's lead. Circuits became shorter, surfaces were improved,

reconnaissance and practice laps, which had been introduced very early on, now became vital as competition was revived.

The first post-war Grand Prix had been held in 1921, for cars complying with the American-inspired 3-litre capacity limit. From 1922–25 a 2-litre limit was applied, and after the 1924 season riding mechanics were banned. Several had been killed or seriously injured, and shorter circuits and improved puncture resistance in tyres made them largely a deadweight sop to tradition.

With their removal, rear-view mirrors became obligatory, and the cars had to retain two seats, with a minimum body width of about 2ft 6in. The cars of this period were increasingly low-slung, with the driver seated on the floor and his legs stretched out rather than hanging down to reach the pedals.

In 1926 a new 1500cc Formula was introduced, and it ran into 1927 when the mandatory second seat requirement was discontinued and the Grand Prix cars of the time became 'offset single-seaters'. Then came the Depression years, in which virtual Formule Libre reigned. Manufacturers and private owners raced whatever cars they could afford, and from 1931–1933 the only stipulations made for Grand Prix races governed their duration. In 1931 they had to last at least ten hours, which required driver pairings as in the long-distance sports car events which had become so popular, and in 1932 this figure was relaxed to 'between five and ten hours'. In 1933 race distance was pegged at a minimum of 500 kilometres, or 312 miles, and then for 1934 a proper set of Grand Prix regulations returned.

This was the dawn of the 750-kilogramme maximum weight Formula which was to see the state-promoted German teams of Mercedes-Benz and Auto Union crushing all opposition with their sophisticated independently-suspended chassis and extremely powerful engines.

They were the mightiest Grand Prix cars ever seen in motor racing history, and from 1938–39 a new Formula was introduced, to reduce the speeds which they had attained. The new Formula stipulated a *minimum* weight limit of 850kg, a limit of 3 litres capacity for supercharged engines and of $4\frac{1}{2}$ litres for unsupercharged engines. While the German teams continued their domination, the great Italian marques contented themselves with racing $1\frac{1}{2}$-litre supercharged Voiturettes against each other.

Meanwhile the Formule Libre events of the Depression years had seen Alfa Romeo successfully introducing the classic single-seat, centrally disposed, racing car layout to Grand Prix racing, and with this development much of the modern racing driver's environment had been assembled; the single-seat central driving position; short, often artificial circuit; practice; pit stops and pit signals . . . it was all there.

Motor racing between the wars was dominated first by Italy then by France before the pendulum swung back to the Italians and then moved on to Germany.

Pietro Bordino was one of the first of the great Italians of this period; a long-serving Fiat employee who had ridden as mechanic to Nazzaro, Lancia and DePalma pre-war. At 18 he had made his driving debut, on a FIAT, in the 1908 Chateau Thierry hill-climb, and had won it outright. After the war Bordino achieved full stature, leading the Brescia Grand Prix and the French Grand Prix in 1921–22 before scoring two great wins at Monza, including the first Italian Grand Prix.

He had a frustrating time in succeeding years as he led races regularly, but his cars failed, and when Fiat finally withdrew from racing Bordino's career seemed finished. He turned to Bugatti, and in 1928 was practising for the Circuit of Alessandria race in northern Italy when a dog galloped into his path. The hapless animal jammed the Bugatti's steering and it crashed through railings to topple into the River Tanaro. Pietro Bordino was pinned beneath the wreck, and drowned. . . .

Meanwhile, Alfa Romeo's fortunes had risen with those of Antonio Ascari. Born in 1888, this tough, practical man set up a motor business in Milan which became the Alfa Romeo agency for Lombardy. He began racing in 1919, with a pre-war Grand Prix Fiat he had prepared himself, and immediately leapt to fame by winning national hill-climbs. Later that year he led the Targa Florio, and then found his way through his agency into the Alfa Romeo factory team.

When Alfa introduced their P2 Grand Prix car in 1924 Ascari led the French Grand Prix (his first race outside Italy) until his car's engine failed with two laps to run. His car failed again in the dying laps of the Targa Florio — when he was leading — but everything held together under his forceful driving at Monza, where he won the Italian Grand Prix.

In 1925 Ascari proved his newfound ability to drive fast and still preserve his car when he won the inaugural Belgian Grand Prix at Spa.

He was the standard-setter of his time when, on July 26, 1925, he stormed into the lead of the French Grand Prix at Montlhéry. When a light drizzle began to coat the circuit he refused to ease up, and then slid wide on a fast curve, ran into a paling fence and sustained fatal injuries as the Alfa Romeo rolled over and over . . . it was to be 20 years before the name Ascari re-emerged.

While the Italians dominated the sport, Sunbeam in England produced 'Fiats in Green Paint' which brought fame to one great British driver — Major Henry O'Neal de Hane Segrave.

An ex-Etonian wartime pilot, Segrave had shot down a German Aviatik scout 'plane before his own DH2 was downed, and later his FE8 was shot down from 7000 feet by anti-aircraft fire. Segrave survived with silver plates in one foot, and a permanent limp.

He was posted to America as an aviation attaché and his enthusiasm for motor racing was sparked there by a chance meeting with Bill Bruce-Brown, brother of the great American driver.[*]

Back in England after the war, Segrave charmed his way into the Sunbeam works team, and in 1923 his steady, reasoned 'win at the lowest

18

*David Bruce-Brown—see page 28.

Above: Antonio
Ascari brings his
Alfa Romeo P2
into the pits after
winning the 1924
Italian Grand Prix,
to be greeted by the
mechanics and his
young son Alberto

Right: Antonio
Ascari with his Alfa
Romeo teammate
Giuseppe Campari
after victory in the
1924 French Grand
Prix. (Ascari was
leading when his
engine failed three
laps before the end)

possible speed' approach brought them victory in the French Grand Prix at Tours. It was the last major success for a British car and driver until 1957. . . .

Segrave retired from racing in 1927, with 31 wins to his credit from 49 starts, and that year saw him become the first man to exceed 200 mph on land when he set a new Land Speed Record in the 1000 hp Sunbeam *Slug* on Daytona Beach. In 1929 he raised the record to over 231 mph in the Irving-Napier *Golden Arrow* and within two weeks his power boat *Miss England* beat American ace Gar Wood in a major Floridan race.

King George knighted Segrave for these achievements, and he enjoyed a deliriously triumphant homecoming. But 15 months later he was dead, killed on Friday, June 13, 1930, when his new boat, *Miss England II*, smashed into an underwater obstruction while attacking the World Water Speed Record on Lake Windermere.

While Segrave was Britain's much-loved 'Knight of Speed', Robert Benoist and Louis Chiron had become the toast of France. The former, another wartime fighter pilot, had won the

French, Spanish, British and Italian Grands Prix for Delage in a shattering 1927 season. The 1½-litre Delage straight-eights were virtually invincible, and Benoist drove them well enough to be almost deified by his countrymen, but when Louis Delage's empire collapsed so — to some extent — did Benoist's career.

He went eventually to Bugatti, and won the 1937 Le Mans 24-Hours race in one of their cars, shared with Jean-Pierre Wimille. Then came another war with Germany, and Benoist, at 44, was disgusted to find himself rated too old to return to flying. As France was occupied he went 'underground', and led an active resistance cell. He was captured by the Gestapo, and twice escaped, but final betrayal saw the Champion of France taken to the notorious concentration camp at Buchenwald, where he was executed in hideous fashion on August 17, 1944. It was an empty, chillingly futile end for a man whose exploits had thrilled so many. . .

Chiron, happily, was much more fortunate. Born in 1900, this Monegasque driver drove racing cars from

Major Segrave's 4-litre V12 Sunbeam is pushed away onto Southport sands for his 152·33 mph Land Speed Record run in March, 1926. The car used what was effectively two 2-litre Grand Prix blocks mounted at 75-degrees included angle on a common crankcase

In Boillot's footsteps as Champions of France came Robert Benoist (left) and Jean-Pierre Wimille — seen together after their Bugatti victory in the 1937 Le Mans 24-Hours

1923 to 1955, when he became the oldest driver ever to compete in a World Championship Grand Prix, finishing sixth on his home soil at Monte Carlo in a Lancia.

This stylish, often excitable driver made his name with Bugatti cars before moving to Alfa Romeo and — briefly — to Mercedes-Benz. After the war he returned to the circuits with the ponderous but reliable $4\frac{1}{2}$-litre Lago-Talbots, Maseratis, OSCAs and Lancias plus many, many more.

His best year was 1928 when he won the Italian, Spanish, Rome, San Sebastian and Marne GPs for Bugatti, and his career total of some 30 major race victories includes five French Grands Prix, and three consecutive Czechoslovakian GPs.

Chiron always shone in the arduous Targa Florio, although he never won it, but after a severe crash in one of the difficult Mercedes of 1936 he went into semi-retirement. Later the silver-haired 'Wily Fox', as stylish as ever, scored his last real success in the 1950 Monaco Grand Prix, in which he was third, and then in 1954 he won the Monte Carlo Rally in a Lancia to earn

his final Grand Prix appearance, the following season. For the next two decades the ever spritely Chiron was a debonair part of the scene at the Monaco Grand Prix. . .

While Chiron won the mantle of the greatest 'French' driver of his time there were two Italians who vied for the honour in their own country. They were the cold, deeply-introspective Achille Varzi, and the hot-blooded, fiery and vastly-talented Tazio Nuvolari.

Varzi was 12 years Nuvolari's junior, born in 1904. He was the son of a wealthy textile manufacturer and made his name racing motor cycles before beginning his four-wheeled career with Bugatti cars, running as team-mate to Nuvolari in their private Scuderia.

He felt he was being overshadowed by the older man, and so bought an old P2 Alfa Romeo with which he won four races and a place in the Alfa Romeo works team. But Nuvolari was there with him, and so the darkly untrusting Varzi moved to other teams, first to Maserati and then to Bugatti for three years.

Typical pose for Achille Varzi, scowling, intent, and smoking! He is in an Alfa Romeo Tipo B, having a wheel changed at the Montlhéry pits during the 1934 French GP meeting

He had won the Italian Championship with the P2 in 1930, and shared a Bugatti T51 with Chiron to win the 1931 French Grand Prix before beating Nuvolari in an epic race at Monaco in 1933, again driving for Bugatti. The following year found Varzi back with Alfa Romeo, winning seven major races in the P3 single-seater and adding a superb win in the Mille Miglia.

Then in 1935 he went to drive the rear-engined Auto Union cars and adapted admirably to their tricky handling. This impassive man, peculiarly lacking in any accepted Latin traits, had never had a racing accident until 1936 when a gusty wind threw his Auto Union off the 180 mph straight at Tunis. He miraculously escaped unharmed, but was a slower driver thereafter. He became addicted to cocaine and disappeared into a strange half-life after a brief comeback in 1937–38.

In 1946 Achille Varzi was back in harness, with the Alfa Romeo team. He was now a greying, upright gentleman of 42; mellowed, perhaps more self-assured, certainly warmer than he had been. He was very successful, although not the best postwar driver, and shone in South America. Then in July 1948 he lost control of his

Alfa Romeo on the dank, misty, drizzle-soaked Bremgarten circuit in practice for the Swiss Grand Prix. He died instantly as the car rolled over gently and his linen windcap offered no protection to his head. It was only his second race accident – in a career spanning 20 years. . .

Varzi's complete opposite – in style, manner, temperament and appearance – was Tazio Nuvolari. He was born in 1892, in Ascari country at Casteldario outside Mantua. Bicycle racing was in the family, but the First World War held back Tazio's competition debut until he was nearly 30.

He started on motor cycles in 1920, and in 1921 had his first motor race. He was a colourful, piratical figure in motor-cycling garb and his riding was full of fire, on the ragged edge *all* the time. Observers were already remarking that if he did not kill himself first he would become truly great, and in fact he became probably the greatest driver of all time.

In 1924 Nuvolari was 500 cc Champion of Italy on a Norton. Alfa Romeo gave him a P2 trial drive at Monza in 1925 but he crashed heavily when the gearbox seized. One week later, bandaged and plastered into a

Tazio Giorgio Nuvolari – 'Nivola' – 'Il Campionissimo' – 'The Great Little Man' . . . perhaps the greatest of them all

sitting position, he was lifted onto his Bianchi motor cycle for the *Grand Prix des Nations*, which he won in streaming rain!

This was the first of many such episodes which made him a living legend, and he concentrated upon racing two-wheelers until 1928 when he formed the Bugatti team with Varzi. After 1930 he abandoned motor-cycle racing and his heyday with Alfa Romeo began. His multiple victories included the Mille Miglia, the Targa Florio, the Italian Grand Prix, the Coppa Ciano, . . . and so the list goes on. Nuvolari excelled in the long Grands Prix of the

time. He excelled in shorter minor events. He excelled on high-speed artificial tracks. He excelled on the most tortuous of road circuits. He simply excelled everywhere, in anything.

Nuvolari moved to Maserati when the ageing Alfas proved too frail in 1933, and then flitted around to Bugatti, back to Maserati and then to Alfa Romeo once more in 1935. He invigorated a team dispirited and crushed by German might and his eight major wins that season included a desperately hard-fought German Grand Prix which humbled the Nazi

teams on their own soil.

It was a classic battle against seemingly impossible odds — just the situation in which the bronzed, wiry little man with the long yellow teeth revelled. His indomitable spirit, fearless daring and spectacular style endeared him to the crowds, and he was always a formidable opponent, no matter what car he was driving.

Early in 1938 'Nivola' suffered burns when his Alfa Romeo 308 burst into flames in practice at Pau. He swore he would never drive for them again, and turned to Auto Union. He adapted perfectly to the rear-engined cars' quirky handling and he won the last two great races of the season. In 1939 it was fitting that Nuvolari, the spirit of the age, should win the Belgrade Grand Prix on the day war was declared and mainstream motor racing spluttered to a halt.

After the war the 54-year-old ace returned, but now he was suffering an incurable lung affliction, aggravated by fuel and exhaust fumes to the extent of making him choke blood.

He drove with a surgical mask covering his nose and mouth, hiding

Left: Nuvolari's D-Type Auto Union bellows down one of Donington's curving 'straights' during the 1938 GP, which it won. The Italian ace was driving with cracked ribs tightly strapped after hitting a stag in practice

Below, left: Rudolf Caracciola – the great Mercedes ace of the 1920s and 1930s; an aloof character, conscious of his talent and position

Below: Swing axles and V16 horsepower taking charge as Bernd Rosemeyer spins his Auto Union C-Type at Monaco in 1936. This was a fairly common experience for the ex-motor cyclist, but he ended the season as European Champion

the intense personal sorrow of having lost both his sons in their youth as much as protecting his delicate health. But still 'The Little Man' was a winner, and his Maserati, Cisitalia and Ferrari cars were always to be feared as he turned-in some epic drives. Only towards the very end did he begin to be used by race promoters as his powers waned.

In 1950 he won the 1½-litre class at the Monte Pelligrino hill-climb in a Cisitalia, and that was to be his last race. On August 11, 1953 – soon after his 61st birthday – Tazio Giorgio Nuvolari – the most revered man in motor racing history – died in his bed in Mantua. To the last he had never given up, and he can never be forgotten. . .

Only one man came close to toppling Nuvolari from his throne as the best driver of his time, regardless of the cars he drove. This was Rudolf Caracciola, the great Mercedes-Benz *fahrer* who won six German Grands

Prix – five of them on the arduous Nürburgring looped around the Eifel Mountains – and 23 other top-line International races between 1926 and 1939.

Caracciola was born in 1901, the son of a successful hotelier from Remagen on the Rhine. He worked for the Fafnir motor works, where he was introduced to motor racing, and then joined Mercedes and began sprinting and hill-climbing their cars in 1924.

They entered him in the first German Grand Prix, on the AVUS track in Berlin, in 1926, and his sensitive wet-weather skills brought one of the notoriously dangerous 2-litre Mercedes home in first place despite incessant rain.

Caracciola grew up with Mercedes' vast 7·1-litre sports-cum-Formule Libre SSK cars, winning the 1928 German Grand Prix under a blistering sun, winning the German race again and the Mille Miglia in 1931 and then

going to Alfa Romeo when Mercedes withdrew from racing.

When Alfa in turn withdrew their works team in 1933, Caracciola joined forces with his close friend, Louis Chiron, to form the Scuderia CC, running private Alfas. In practice for his first race, at Monaco, Caracciola crashed heavily and smashed his thigh.

This injury was to trouble him for the rest of his life. He limped, it gave him constant pain, and he was liable to tire quickly, but his cool, commanding skill and supreme wet weather ability stood him in good stead as he led the Mercedes-Benz teams 1934–1939.

Like Nuvolari he suffered personal tragedy, his first wife Charly being killed under an avalanche at Arosa in the winter of 1933–34 while his thigh was still healing. He remarried (Alice) in 1937 and in those years of the 750-Kilogramme Formula he won 16 major races, including the French, Belgian, Monaco, Swiss, German, Italian and Czechoslovakian Grands Prix.

He was Champion of Europe in 1930–32, 1935–38, and in the new 3-litre Formula he continued winning, although past his peak, and two wins and a string of second places in 1938 gave him his third European title.

But at last his authority within the German team was being challenged. He was still very fast, but no longer the fastest, and as former mechanic Hermann Lang came to prominence the declining, rather snobbish Caracciola became more testy, more secretive and demanding.

When Caracciola won his sixth, and last, German Grand Prix in 1939 he was still indisputably a very great racing driver, although past his peak, and he then spent the war years in neutral Switzerland, and became a naturalised Swiss citizen.

In 1946 he was invited to Indianapolis, but he crashed one of Joel Thorne's Specials in a trial run, apparently after being struck in the face by a bird. He was unconscious for 11 days and recovered very slowly from severe concussion. When Mercedes returned to competition in 1950–51 they invited the ageing maestro to rejoin their team. He was a joyous fourth in the 1952 Mille Miglia, but that May in a sports car race at Berne his 300SL smashed into a tree when the rear brakes locked, and Caracciola broke his thigh once more. It was the end of a great career, and in 1959 Rudolf Caracciola died in a Kassel clinic, victim of an infectious jaundice which developed into cirrhosis. . .

Dick Seaman had a terrific 1936 season with this Giulio Ramponi-modified ex-Howe Delage, then basically ten years old. Here he is on his way to winning the JCC '200' at Donington Park. His exploits in the Delage won him a Mercedes-Benz works drive

The American Way

While most of western Europe was boiling with competition fervour, America's first motoring competition was a decidedly dull and deadly earnest affair organised by the *Chicago Times-Herald*, in November, 1895. A snow-affected race was followed by searching laboratory tests which provide a superb record of the early cars' power but which befuddled the readership of the *Times-Herald* no end.

In 1896 further damage was done to the embryo 'sport' by the New York *Cosmopolitan* race. This contemporary report tells what happened:

'Six horseless carriages, entered for a drive,
Wheel came off one, then there were five;
Five horseless carriages, racing as before,
Chain slipped on one, and then there were four;
Four horseless carriages, speeding merrily,
Bicycle ran into one, and then there were three;
Three horseless carriages, came to a hill,
Hill stayed right where it was, so the drivers had to get off and push, and that was why the time between City Hall and Irvington for the prize of 3000 dollars offered by a magazine was not what it might have been had there not been any hill there!'

That same year saw the first track race, run over five laps of a one-mile dirt course at Narragansett Park, Cranston, Rhode Island as an attraction at the Rhode Island State Fair. The winner was A. H. Whiting, whose Riker electric car averaged 24 mph to beat seven other competitors.

Although it was not realised at the time, this was the way American automobile racing was to develop. Sprints and hill-climbs and trials abounded, but there were no great road races on anything like the European scale until 1904, when the first race for the Vanderbilt Trophy was run on Long Island.

William K. Vanderbilt was a millionaire enthusiast who founded a race between national teams on Gordon Bennett lines. But every Vanderbilt Cup was to be on American soil, and it brought some American drivers to International prominence.

One of these was George Heath, a native Long Islander who preferred to live in Paris, where he is believed to have run a tailor's shop. He had raced Panhards as early as 1898, and stayed with the *Grand Marque* thereafter, winning both the Ardennes race and the first Vanderbilt Cup in tigrish style in 1904. His later outings were highlighted by second place in the second Vanderbilt Cup race, but thereafter he faded into obscurity.

Joe Tracy, on the other hand, was an Irish immigrant — born in County Waterford in 1873 — who had come to America at the age of 19. He trained as a steam engineer and then began driving Panhard, Richard-Brasier and Renault cars for private owners.

The Automobile Club of America selected him to represent them in the 1905 Gordon Bennett race around the Auvergne Mountains in France, but his fearsome 17·7-litre Locomobile damaged its transmission on the run from Le Havre to Clermont. Back home Tracy came third in the Vanderbilt Cup race to score his adopted country's best-yet International placing.

In 1906 he won the Eliminating Trial

to choose the American Vanderbilt team, but in the race itself his Locomobile simply ate its tyres, and after setting the fastest time on one rare change-free lap, Tracy skidded into some spectators and injured a small boy. He retired from racing thereafter to become a consultant engineer, and he pioneered antique car preservation before his death in 1959.

In 1908 the American Automobile Association ran the Vanderbilt Cup to a virtual free formula, while the rival ACA abided by new European regulations and organised their first American Grand Prize race on a road circuit outside the old Southern city of Savannah, Georgia.

The European teams flocked there instead of to Long Island, where the all-American Vanderbilt Cup race fell to George Robertson's Locomobile, 'Old No 16'. This victory made Robertson the first American to win the nation's classic road race in an American car, and the 24-year-old garage owner's son from New York became a national celebrity.

New Yorkers already knew how good this dashing young man could be (in the right company) for he had already won a 24-Hour race at Brighton Beach, NY, on a Simplex, and he had added another win in the Fairmount Park 200 at Philadelphia, with a Locomobile.

After his Vanderbilt success he drove for two more seasons, until the 1910 Cup race — the last on the dangerous, difficult-to-police Long Island course — when he appeared as captain of the Benz team and suffered a dreadful crash while showing the circuit to a newspaper reporter. His injuries put an end to his racing days.

In 1917 Robertson went to France as Transport Controller for the American Expeditionary Force, and in 1921 he managed the Duesenberg team which won the French Grand Prix. He died in 1955.

While the Vanderbilt Cup series declined, the Grand Prize races saw a new young star flash brilliantly onto the American racing scene, and all too quickly burn out. This was David Bruce-Brown, born to a wealthy New York society family in 1890.

He was a rugged, broad-shouldered, smiling young man who had talked his way into the driving seat of a record-breaking FIAT on Daytona's Ormond

David Bruce-Brown — the youthful American society ace whose exploits with the giant chain-driven Fiats made him a living legend before the First World War. Here he is pictured at Dieppe before the 1912 Grand Prix in which he led at the end of the first day by over 2 minutes from Boillot. On the second day he was disqualified

Beach in 1908. He was only 18, but he shattered W. K. Vanderbilt's four-year-old mile record by 3-seconds.

Many successes followed, and when Bruce-Brown joined the Benz team for the Grand Prize race at Savannah in 1910 he *won*, beating team-mate Victor Hemery by 1·42 seconds in the process! In 1911, driving for FIAT, he was third in the inaugural Indianapolis 500 Mile race and he won the Grand Prize once more. In 1912 he led the French Grand Prix by miles before adding fuel to his FIAT away from the pits after a feed pipe had broken, and being duly disqualified.

That October found America's 22-year-old ace preparing to defend his American Grand Prize title, at Milwaukee. In practice the big FIAT's rear tyre blew out, the car plunged into a ditch and somersaulted, and Bruce-Brown was hurled to his tragic death.

Ralph DePalma took over Bruce-Brown's crown as America's leading all-round racing driver. He had come to America in 1893 as a wide-eyed 10-year-old Italian immigrant, and in 1908 he had started racing Allen-Kingston cars on New York's dirt tracks. Later that year he made his big-time debut with a FIAT at Savannah, and late in 1911 he first appeared in a Mercedes which brought him the National Championship in 1912, clinched in the Vanderbilt Cup race at the Milwaukee meeting 'for David'. Two days later he crashed heavily and was severely injured on the last lap of the Grand Prize.

DePalma was intensely capable, jut-chinned and strong minded, and in 1914 he won his second National Championship with a Grand Prix-type Mercedes, and used the car to win at Indianapolis in 1915 and to score a string of further race wins in 1916.

During the war years he worked as an aero engineer with Packard, and then went into the 1920s with Ballot. He was placed second in the 1921 French Grand Prix, with his nephew Peter DePaolo as his riding mechanic (DePaolo was later to become a National Champion in his own right).

After that 1921 season, DePalma lived off his reputation rather than adding materially to it, taking part in a series of showman races with little competitive point. When the Depression put the squeeze on these exhibi-

Contemporary track conditions are pictured graphically in this shot of Ralph de Palma's Ballot at Le Mans during the 1921 French Grand Prix. Just to annoy Ernest Ballot the patrician naturalised American held back early on, and finished second to Murphy's winning Duesenberg. The riding mechanic is Peter de Paolo

tion events, Ralph DePalma joined Mobil Oil as a consultant, and stayed with them until his death in 1956.

One of America's most beloved early drivers — and the one most detested by DePalma — was Berna Eli Oldfield; bluff cigar-chewing showman, 'King of the Barnstormers'. Born in 1877, he first gained fame in 1902 when he drove Henry Ford's famous '999' to many sprint wins. He tried his hand at road racing and top-class track racing without conspicuous success and was happier in match races, exhibition events and gaudy promotional stunts. Until 1918 he was happy to perform as a very big fish in a rather small pond, and his earnings proved

Marmon in Indianapolis in 1908 when he heard that a new $2\frac{1}{2}$-mile Motor Speedway was being built there and when it opened in 1909 he won several events in Marmon cars.

He was National Champion in 1910, and wanted to retire while at the top to concentrate on his engineering career. Howard Marmon talked him instead into doing just one more race, the inaugural '500', and they built a single-seater Marmon Six for the occasion.

Harroun fitted the car with probably the first-ever rear-view mirror to compensate for the lack of a riding mechanic, and early in the long race he nosed the Marmon *Wasp* as it was known through the field from 28th to

that a wise choice. He retired from driving to form his own tyre company in 1918, and four years later sold out to Firestone. By this time he was reckoned to be a multi-millionaire, and he then lost most of his fortune in the stock market crash of 1929, and worked as a consulting engineer until his death in 1946. Oldfield's name is prominent in American motor racing history, but as a 'great driver' he was hardly worth a light. . .

A man who does deserve to be remembered is Ray Harroun, for like Ferenc Szisz he was a mechanic-cum-engineer who won the first running of a classic race series — the inaugural Indianapolis 500 Miles race. Born in 1879, Harroun began racing on Chicago's dirt track in 1905, joined

fifth place. While he rested briefly, Cyrus Patschke took over to steal second place, and then Harroun attained the lead when Mulford's Lozier lost two laps in the pits, and held it to the end of the race. He remained in automotive engineering for the rest of his working life, and died in 1968 as another race-driving octogenarian — he was 89.

The building of Indianapolis had firmly orientated America towards enclosed track racing. The crowd could see everything that happened, they could be well marshalled, and 'freebies' were cut down by boundary fences and hawk-eyed ticket-sellers.

At Atlanta, Asa Chandler and Ed Durant built an oval race-track with a loose gravel surface, and in Cali-

Engineer-driver Ray Harroun in the Marmon 6 single-seater in which he was credited with victory in the inaugural Indianapolis 500 in 1911. The rearview mirror was one of the earliest ever fitted on a motor car, and was necessary because Harroun and his relief driver Cyrus Patschke had no riding mechanic to keep watch

fornia former cycling fan Fred Moscovics promoted enormous velo-drome-type board tracks, big enough to carry cars.

So Playa del Rey, just outside Los Angeles, sprouted a high-banked, mile-long oval board speedway, and it paid its way handsomely until one fateful day in 1913 when the great wooden wonder burned to the ground.

Its example was taken-up by promoters right across America, and between 1910 and 1931 the nation saw 24 of these wooden ovals come and go. Their highly-specialised structures rumbled and flexed beneath the potent racing machinery of a burgeoning American industry, breeding slim-

at Beverley Hills, and rapidly made such a reputation for himself that he was named Duesenberg team captain for their onslaught on the revived French Grand Prix, in 1921.

With Ernie Olson as his mechanic, Murphy ignored the rib-crushing effects of a practice somersault to rip around the rough, stone-strewn Le Mans course to beat the best that Europe could offer, averaging no less than 78·22 mph for 321 miles.

Back in America he began racing his Grand Prix Duesy with a Miller engine, and won the Indianapolis 500 in 1922 on his way to the National Championship. He lost the crown the following year, but only when a trip to

Jimmy Murphy, the Irish-American track star, delighted after winning the 1921 French Grand Prix at Le Mans. His ribs were strapped after a practice somersault in a sister Duesenberg. Note the crack in the Duesenberg body, after its 322-mile battering

bodied, soon single-seater, cars whose highly supercharged engines could be run flat-out for long distances. While Indianapolis maintained its aura by offering the richest money in motor racing, it was the boards which fed Indy with talent and ingenuity.

One of the track stars who made his name equally in road racing was Jimmy Murphy, a tough, uncompromising, fiercely competitive Irish-American. Orphaned as a child he had quickly learned to live on his wits, found a job in a Californian racing garage and at 21 became riding mechanic in the Duesenberg team. On Labour Day, 1919 he made his driving debut on the boards at Altoona, Pa, and crashed.

Five months later he beat the stars

the Italian Grand Prix made him miss some qualifying rounds. He was a close runner-up to Eddie Hearne, and was grimly determined to regain the crown in 1924. He did so, but late in the season he tangled with Phil Shafer while battling for the lead on the dirt at Syracuse, NY, and crashed fatally — a board safety rail piercing his heart.

In his earliest days, Murphy had been riding mechanic in Tommy Milton's Duesenberg, and 'The Great Milton' was one of the greatest of all track aces. Born in 1893, Milton had a furious will to win. He added considerable skill to the courage to race despite the handicap of being blind from birth in one eye.

He had started with a barnstorming troupe in 1914, but walked out when the scripted aces were disgruntled at his regularly beating them. Immediately after the war he became Duesenberg's team captain, and won the 301-mile Elgin road race by a margin of 24 *minutes*! One week later he was hospitalised and in danger of losing a leg, through critical burns sustained when leading a race on the high boards of Uniontown, Pa.

In hospital he completed designs for a twin-engined record car, and in April 1920 he drove it at 156 mph on Daytona Beach. He won the National Championship that season, and became the first man to retain his crown, in 1921, when he also won at Indy.

In 1923 he became the first man to win a second '500', in an HCS-Miller, and two years later he led the Italian Grand Prix briefly before his Duesenberg fell back to finish fourth. After his retirement Milton served the sport for many years, and died in 1962, aged 69.

Frank Lockhart was a different character. He was simply a genius — a natural-born driver and engineer. Born in 1902, in Dayton, Ohio, he was slow academically, never properly literate, but was fascinated by things mechanical.

By the time he was 16 he had built himself a Fronty-Ford, in which he began racing and winning on the Californian tracks. In 1926 he went to Indy, took over Pete Kreis' Miller for the race when Kreis fell ill, and was flagged off as winner of the '500' when rain fell after 400 miles. The kid was five miles ahead of the field, and had made himself a star overnight. . .

Later that year, Lockhart fitted supercharger intercoolers to his car, and used their efficiency to punish opponents severely on the boards. He kept the invention secret for long months as he scored win after win, and at Indianapolis he led for 300 miles until a con-rod broke. He promptly sat down and designed a replacement, which never broke.

Later in 1927 he took his highly-modified Miller '91' to Muroc Dry Lake and clocked a speed of 171·02 mph. The only faster car at that time was a Land Speed Record monster, and with the Miller engine doubled-up, in a suitably streamlined shell, Lockhart knew he could become the fastest man on earth.

Stutz sponsored the project, and Lockhart took his car onto Daytona Beach on a grey squally day in February, 1928. His first attempt on the record of 206 mph failed, when the car picked-up soft sand, skipped into the ocean and half-drowned its driver.

On April 25, 1928, a second attempt ended in total disaster when a clam shell slit a tyre at over 210 mph, and the delicate little Stutz rampaged end-over-end, hurling out Frank Lockhart's lifeless body at the end of its gyrations. He was barely 25.

That same year saw a driver named Louis Meyer winning the prestigious '500', and it was the first of his three victories in the track classic — a feat which he pioneered.

All Meyer's 12 years of racing centred on Indy. He had been mechanic to Frank Elliott in 1926, and when Wilbur Shaw bought one of Elliott's cars for the 1927 '500', Meyer co-drove it into fourth place. For 1928 he received backing from truck manufacturer Alden L. Sampson, and he won his first '500', following up with more successes which brought him the National Championship title. In 1929 the tough, experienced ex-mechanic was second to Ray Keech at Indianapolis and retained his title.

As the Depression bit deep, Meyer had three lean years, and then in 1933 he won at the Speedway for the second time and took his third National Championship.

His third victory in the 500-mile classic followed in 1936, and he retired after the 1939 race in which he crashed with only three of the 200 laps remaining.

Thereafter Louis Meyer devoted his considerable talents to race engine development, going into partnership with Dale Drake in 1946 to buy Fred Offenhauser's engine plant. Meyer-Drake Offenhauser engines powered every winning Indy car for 18 years commencing in 1947, and the partnership finally broke-up in 1964, when Meyer moved to Ford to produce their V8 track-racing engines. He is still

Frank Lockhart's breathtaking Stutz Black Hawk 'beach car' at Daytona in February, 1928. His runs ended in a crash into the surf. Later in the year the Stutz crashed at perhaps 220 mph when a clam shell cut a too-fragile rear tyre — and at 26 Lockhart was dead

Daytona Beach Florida February 1928.

close to the USAC scene today. . .

Only one man emulated Meyer's three-win Indianapolis 500 record in this 'tween-wars period, and that was Wilbur Shaw — the man who became America's 'Mr Motor Racing'.

Born in 1903, Shaw was a native-born Hoosier, and was Indy-struck from his earliest years. He dreamed of racing in the '500' and of winning it; he fought his way into dirt-track racing and in 1927 made his Indy debut, with Lou Meyer.

He ran with the leaders in several dirt events later that year but then his world was shattered by the death of his wife in childbirth. Unable to find form on Championship circuits in 1928 he returned to the unsanctioned half-mile dirt ovals. He slowly regained stability, remarried and rejoined the Championship scene in 1929, after being barred from the '500' for his 'pirate' racing activities. He immediately won six of the first seven 100-mile dirt events in which he ran.

Shaw's Indianapolis record was undistinguished until 1933, when he was second, and in 1935 he was second again. Apart from two forays into the revived Vanderbilt Cup race on New York's Roosevelt Raceway, Shaw concentrated purely on the Indianapolis race thereafter.

In 1937 he achieved his ambition, winning in the Offy-engined Gilmore Special, and in 1938 he was second yet again, in the same car. For 1939 entrant Mike Boyle bought him a Grand Prix 3-litre Maserati 8CTF from Italy, and this machine was vastly superior to its opponents, setting new standards on 'The Brickyard' and carrying Wilbur Shaw to his second and third '500' victories in 1939 and 1940.

Nobody had yet won the '500' four times, and in 1941 Shaw was driving the Maserati towards that elusive victory when with 49 laps remaining its right-side rear wheel failed and put the car into the wall.

With America at war, Shaw worked with Firestone's aviation division, and when peace returned he was the man who saved the Indianapolis Motor Speedway from dereliction and persuaded local businessman Anton Hulman to buy it. Shaw became President and General Manager, and his promotional abilities were thereafter devoted to the 500-mile race which had made him a national celebrity. Perhaps his fine machinery enhanced his true driving skill, but to most Americans Wilbur Shaw *was* automobile racing, and his untimely death in a light aircraft crash outside Decatur on October

WINNER
WILBUR SHAW (driver) JIGGER JOHNSON (mech)
Indianapolis Motor Speedway
1937

30, 1954, caused nationwide sorrow.

Shaw's type of racing, the American left-turn only track race, seems hopelessly undemanding and dull to Europeans nurtured on road racing. Perhaps from the aspect of pure driving skill this is true — perhaps it is not — but certainly track racing could be desperately demanding with many starters using very fast cars, jammed together in close company on extremely tight circuits. Clouds of dust and debris flew around on the dirt tracks, while in the furious days of board track racing — particularly towards the end of their careers — the cars' slipstreams carried devastating showers of hurtling, needle-sharp wood splinters. It was a type of racing unknown, and largely unimagined, in Europe, and there was one driver who both typified the spirit of this type of American racing, and yet who went some way towards bridging the widening gulf between it and European-style road racing.

He was bluff, genial Rex Mays. Born in 1915, he was like an ammeter — he showed maximum charge, all the time! There was little science or sympathy in much of his driving, but his indomitable 'have a go' spirit endeared him to the fans.

Mays learned his trade with modified stock cars in California, and made his Indianapolis debut in 1934. Thereafter he contested eleven more '500s', led the race in nine of them and twice finished second — in 1940 and 1941. Four times he qualified on pole position, and as long as his car held together his foot was hard down — it was the only way he knew.

Many of his dirt-track records remained unbeaten for years, and in 1937 he drove his road-racing Alfa Romeo into third place behind the German cars in the Vanderbilt Cup. He was the first American home, and the Grand Prix contingent suddenly sat up and realised that some track-trained drivers could also turn right.

In 1940–41 Rex Mays won two consecutive National Championship titles, emulating the earlier achievements of Tommy Milton and Louis Meyer, and after the war he was quickly back in harness. He was third in the Championship in 1948, but it was to be his last full season, for in 1949 he crashed fatally on the Del Mar dirt track, in California. It was a tragic end for a driver who totally exemplified America's spirited and dauntless brand of motor racing.

America's 'Mr Speedway' — Wilbur Shaw with Jigger Johnson in the 1937 Gilmore Special which they crewed to victory in the Indianapolis 500. Note the surface of 'The Brickyard', and the crash helmets then so strange to European eyes

34

Birth of the Championship

When motor racing got under way again in Europe after the Second World War, two full seasons of 'anything goes' racing were followed by a new Grand Prix Formula introduced in 1948. This was a combination of the 1½-litre supercharged Voiturette regulations, which the Italians had used happily in the late 1930s, and the unsupercharged 4½-litre class from the Grand Prix field.

It was a sensible choice, enabling existing cars from the pre-war years to be developed and uprated. Nobody wielded their ten year-old cars more effectively than *Alfa Corse* — the official Alfa Romeo team — and in these dying years of the turbulent 1940s it was a French driver who set the standard behind the wheel of the Italian cars.

The driver was Jean-Pierre Wimille, an austere, rather aloof, often withdrawn man, quite out of character with his Parisian background. The son of a journalist, born in 1908, he jumped directly into good class motor racing in 1930 when he drove a Bugatti in the French Grand Prix at Pau. Early in 1931 he was second in the Monte Carlo Rally, and later that year he shared the fourth place Bugatti in the Italian Grand Prix with Jean Gaupillat.

In these early days Wimille was wild, showing more dash than judgement. He scored his first win at Oran in a brand new twin overhead camshaft Bugatti Type 51, and then turned to Alfa Romeo and won the Lorraine GP at Nancy in an ageing *Monza* model. By 1934 he was in the Bugatti team, winning at Algiers despite the marque's increasing obsolescence, and in 1936 he won the sports car French Grand Prix with Raymond Sommer, sharing a vast Bugatti 57S. His single-seat Bugatti was second in the American Vanderbilt Cup race, and in 1937 he and Robert Benoist won at Le Mans. Wimille again won Le Mans for Bugatti, with Pierre Veyron, in 1939; when France was occupied 'J-P' served with the French Resistance.

Jean-Pierre Wimille was acknowledged to be the greatest driver of his time in the late-1940s, notably with Alfa Romeo. Still French blue meant much to him, and here at Lausanne his Simca-Gordini *Voiturette* leads an Italian Cisitalia D46. He crashed fatally in a similar Simca at Buenos Aires in January, 1949

The very first postwar motor race meeting was held in the Bois de Boulogne, Paris, in September 1945, and Wimille was the very popular winner of its major event, in the old 4·7-litre single-seat Bugatti.

In 1946 he campaigned his own ancient Alfa Romeo 308 with great success, and joined the works team for the *Grand Prix des Nations* in Geneva. He was third in the final, after winning his heat.

During 1947 and 1948 he achieved full stature as a driver, completing an Argentine tour with a Gordini and his own Alfa in 1948. He had won the Belgian and Swiss Grands Prix in his first full season with *Alfa Corse*, and in 1948 he set the driving standards of his time to win the French and Italian Grands Prix, the Monza Autodrome GP celebrating the track's re-opening, the Turin race and the Rosario GP in Argentina. He was the best.

He had many fans in the South American country, one of whom we shall meet shortly, and he returned there early in 1949 to drive a tiny 1430 cc Simca-Gordini — a French-built car, which was important to him.

In early morning practice for the Buenos Aires Grand Prix the blue car suddenly veered off-line in a tight corner, smashed into a roadside tree, and killed its 41-year-old driver. Some say Wimille was dazzled by the morning sun, others that his loose scarf blew over his eyes, but all agreed that he was quite irreplaceable. To some extent they were wrong. . .

In preparation for the 1950 season, the International governing body of the sport announced a brand-new Grand Prix competition, a World Championship incorporating the classic races.

A graduated points scale was to be applied, and so the motor racing competition was born which more than any other has captured the imagination of the general public. In its first 27 seasons, 15 men became World Champion racing driver. Not all can be recalled as all-time greats; some greater men have never won the Championship, but we shall look first at those who combined Champion status with the unique ability to set the driving standards of their time. Of these, none were greater than Juan Manuel Fangio . . .

Fangio's 6-cylinder Chevrolet Coupe bought for his Carrera racing by the people of his home town of Balcarce. At the age of 29 he drove this car to win the 1940 *Gran Premio Internacional del Norte* — his first major success

Opposite, lower: Fangio trying a 2-litre Formula 2 Ferrari for size at Monza in 1949 when he won the Autodrome GP in this car. The ACA had been so delighted with his Maserati Formula 1 performances earlier in the season that they bought him this car for Formula 2

Juan Manuel Fangio
BORN JUNE 24, 1911, BALCARCE, BUENOS AIRES PROVINCE, ARGENTINA

Five World Drivers' Championship titles; a new record of 24 Championship-qualifying victories from only 51 starts; 28 times on pole position; started all but three of his Grand Prix races from the front row of the grid . . . this is the record which makes the stocky, impassive Argentinian totally unique.

Never were his special skills better demonstrated than in the race which clinched his fifth and final World title, and gave him his record-setting 24th and last Grand Prix victory. It was the German Grand Prix, at the Nürburgring on August 4, 1957.

Fangio, already 46 years old, had won three of the four preceding Championship rounds in his six-cylinder lightweight Maserati 250F. Ranged against him were Maserati's deadly rivals, the Ferrari team which

included the young British tigers, Mike Hawthorn and Peter Collins.

Maserati strategy was unusual. While Ferrari were sending their cars out brimming with fuel to run the 312 miles non-stop, the 250Fs were to start the race lightly-loaded. Fangio hoped that a light car would be suffi-

Alfa Romeo's legendary 'Three Fs' team of 1950 enjoy the Silverstone sun before the first World Championship race of the modern series. Left to right: Luigi Fagioli, Juan Manuel Fangio, Dr Giuseppe Farina

hard, but the maestro had smashed the lap record five times, slashing 12·1 seconds from his 1956 figure!

At the end of lap 12 the bright red Maserati with its yellow nose zoomed into its pit. Fangio, brown-helmeted, cool despite his exertions, stood by impassively as the mechanics struggled to refuel his car and change its rear wheels. They were painfully slow, but the driver stood unmoved by the growing panic around him. Hawthorn and Collins had long gone into the lead when the Maserati was finally ready to go, and then Fangio leapt aboard and exploded out of the pits, wheel-spinning away some 45 seconds behind the fleeing Ferraris.

The two Englishmen took turns to lead, haring round the sun-drenched Nürburgring faster and faster as their fuel loads diminished. For three laps Fangio was held at bay, the Maserati wallowing under its refilled tanks and shiny new tyres. Then the master began to fly . . . and he ate the Englishmen alive.

On lap 16 the gap suddenly closed to 33 seconds. Next time round it was 25·5 seconds. On lap 19 Fangio's hurtling Maserati clipped another 6·1 seconds off the record, and was only 13·5 seconds behind the Ferraris.

The Ferrari pit urged-on their drivers but they were already giving their best against the Old Man, and it wasn't good enough.

Next time round, and Hawthorn led Collins by feet, with Fangio in sight, two seconds astern and closing like an avenging angel. Into the *Nordkehre* behind the pits Fangio nosed his Maserati inside Collins' car, forced it wide and stole second place. He had just ripped another six seconds off the lap record, and eleven off the Englishmen's lead — in one 14-mile lap!

On the way down through the forests to Breidscheid, the Argentinian grand master of motor racing forced by Hawthorn, who never gave up, but hung on grimly to the Maserati for the remaining lap-and-a-half to finish.

Fangio had surpassed himself in a furious display of tigrish virtuosity which won him his 24th Grand Prix,

ciently nimble to give him a long lead before the inevitable fuel stop. If his car could be refuelled rapidly, perhaps he could hold his lead to the finish.

By lap 11 the plan seemed to be working well. The race was half-run and Fangio led Hawthorn and Collins by 27·8 seconds. They were charging

and his fifth World title. The good young'uns shook their heads in disbelief — the Old Man had done it again. . .

Juan Manuel Fangio was the fourth of six children, born on St John's Day, hence his name. His father, Loretto, was a house painter, an immigrant from the Abruzzi in Italy.

Juan was a sickly child, but bright. At 11 he was tinkering with motor cars in Señor Capetini's workshops, and soon after went to work as a mechanic in Viggiano's garage. Football was his passion, and his style earned him his nickname, *El Chueco* ('Bandy-legs').

At 17 he was given his first taste of racing, riding as mechanic in a Señor Ayerza's Chevrolet, which was maintained in the Viggiano garage. The race was a dusty, exciting experience which Fangio never forgot, and after compulsory military service at 21, he returned to Balcarce and opened a small garage of his own, in partnership with Jose Duffard, and dreamed of building his own racing car.

It happened, in 1934: a borrowed Model A Ford, followed by his own modified Model A. But he had little success, even with a fierce Ford V8 Special built with his brother Ruben.

In 1938 Fangio shared Finochietto's *Carretera Turismo* car in the long-distance, open road 'Grand Prix of the Republic', and they were seventh. Balcarce's people began to take an interest in their local racing driver.

They organised a collection to buy him a late-model Chevrolet for this kind of point-to-point racing, but before it could be delivered he drove a battered old Chevy (with Hector Tieri) into fifth place in the 1939 *Gran Premio*. In the Argentine Thousand Mile Race the old Chevrolet lacked horsepower but Fangio ran reliably into third place. Then the Balcarce Chevrolet coupe was delivered at last, and the rapidly improving 29-year-old entered it in the mighty 'International Grand Prix of the North'.

This incredible road race covered 5920 miles, in 13 stages, from Buenos Aires to Lima, Peru, and back. Fangio built up an enormous lead in the early stages, then eased back and allowed his competitors to make faster times without threatening his overall lead. He had learned to win at the slowest possible speed — and it was a lesson he never forgot.

Balcarce's favourite son went on winning these hair-raising open road races into 1941, when wartime restrictions affected the Argentine, and during the next five years he kept himself in trim by taking days away from

Fangio at full noise — power-sliding round Silverstone in his Alfa Romeo 159 in hot pursuit of countryman Gonzalez's winning Ferrari 375. In this classic Geoffrey Goddard picture one can almost hear the Alfa's exhaust note ripping across the aerodrome

his motor business to drive thousands and thousands of miles, on his own, at racing speeds.

In February, 1947, the Péron regime allowed Argentine racing to resume, and Fangio was there, racing Chevrolet Specials and saloons on the short circuits. Varzi and Villoresi were visiting from Europe, and Fangio was intrigued by their elegant, undemonstrative driving styles.

In 1948 they returned, accompanied by Wimille, who was at that time reckoned to be the World's greatest driver. The Argentine Automobile Club bought two Maseratis to oppose them, and Fangio was selected to drive one of these Italian thoroughbreds.

He was introduced to the great Varzi, who freely gave advice on how to handle the nervous, high-powered single-seaters. Fangio later recalled; 'I hung on his every word, scarcely believing my ears; a champion of his class generously giving advice, to a driver as little known as I . . .'

Fangio had similar respect and admiration for Wimille, and the ACA gave him a brief European tour that summer, in which he drove a Simca-Gordini, unsuccessfully, at Reims.

Back home for the 6000-mile Buenos Aires-Caracas race, Fangio selected a close friend, Daniel Urrutia, as his co-driver, but late one night he was caught-out by a deceptive corner near Trujillo, and rolled his car, killing Urrutia. This tragedy was followed quickly by Wimille's death in Buenos Aires, and Fangio only continued racing after much soul-searching.

He was already 38 years old, and now he came good; beating Prince 'Bira' to win the Mar del Plata GP in a Maserati. With Péron's enthusiastic backing, Fangio was despatched to Europe to drive blue-and-yellow Scuderia Argentina Maseratis with Benedetto Campos.

The late Achille Varzi's family gave the team their workshops in which to prepare the cars, and Varzi's faithful mechanic Amedéo Bignami became technical director. With these facilities and know-how the cars were reliable, and with Fangio's uncanny skill they proved immediate winners.

First race was the San Remo GP in Italy. Fangio won. His fans in Argentina, glued to their radios, went berserk with delight . . . and there was more to come.

The rest of that 1949 season was a triumphant succession of victories, at Albi, Marseilles, Monza, Perpignan and Pau before he made his *Grande Epreuve* debut at Spa.

Alfa Romeo had withdrawn from racing that season. The loss of Varzi, of Count Trossi (to cancer) and then of Wimille had left them without drivers. Now they were building a team for the first World Championship season in 1950, and Fangio was invited to join it.

He had an extremely successful season, losing the Championship title only narrowly to team-mate Giuseppe Farina. In 1951 he drove for Alfa Romeo once more, and despite the strong opposition now coming from Ferrari with their unsupercharged $4\frac{1}{2}$-litre cars, he won his first World title.

The Belgian, French and Monaco Grands Prix had fallen to his Alfa Romeo 158 in 1950, and the French, Swiss and Spanish races to his Tipo 159 the following season.

By this time the development potential of the basically pre-war Alfas had been exhausted, and the team withdrew from competition. Fangio drove for Ferrari in the early-season South American races, with great success, and fought with the fiercely powerful and unmanageable V16 BRM in *Formule Libre* events.

The second of these was at Dundrod, in Ulster, and he was to drive a Maserati at Monza the following day. Bad weather caused his onward flight from Paris to Milan to be cancelled, so Fangio drove there overnight. He started the race deceptively tired, and on the second lap his Maserati somersaulted off the Serraglio Bend, hurling Fangio out with a broken neck.

The injury kept him out of racing for the rest of the season, but he returned in 1953 with Maserati, won the Italian Grand Prix and was second several times in a season dominated by Ferrari. In the Mille Miglia he was second again, driving an Alfa Romeo coupe for many miles with only one

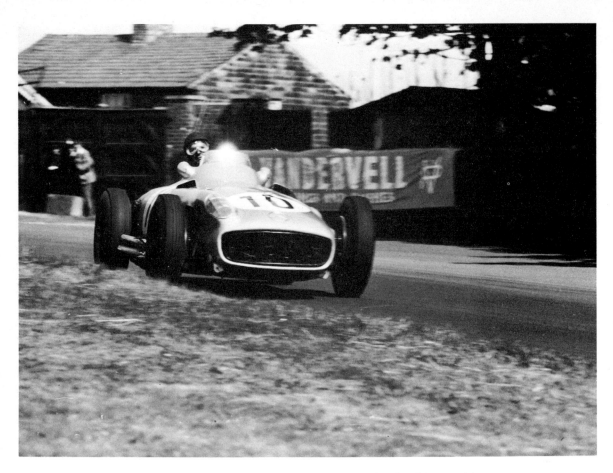

of its front wheels actually steering.

Starting the 1954 season for Maserati, he won the Argentine and Belgian Grands Prix, but Mercedes-Benz were coming back into racing, and they hired the best driver that money could buy, and that was Fangio.

For them he won four more Grand Prix races to take a resounding World Championship title. In 1955 he drove exclusively for the German team and took the Championship once more, and when Mercedes-Benz withdrew he moved to Ferrari for 1956. At the end of the season the Championship lay between Fangio, his youthful team-mate Peter Collins, and Stirling Moss of Maserati. In a logical act at Monza Collins handed over his car to Fangio after the master's own had failed, enabling him to take his fourth title.

For 1957 Fangio returned to Maserati, with whom he had always been happiest since Alfa's withdrawal, and he won the Championship again. Now 47, he won the non-Champion-ship Buenos Aires GP for Maserati in January, 1958, and was fourth in the Argentine Grand Prix. In mid-summer he reappeared at Reims, to take fourth place in the French Grand Prix, and that was to be his last race. His Maserati was ailing near the finish, and Mike Hawthorn's leading Ferrari stormed up onto its tail as Fangio approached the finish line. Hawthorn was about to lap the reigning World Champion, when he braked hard, and allowed Fangio to cross the line first. It was a chivalrous gesture which moved Fangio deeply, and a fitting mark of respect from the man who was to take over his Championship crown.

Fangio retired at the top of the pile. He never knew the bitterness or regret of being a dethroned Champion, and although he had been beaten he had never, ever, been outdriven in a Grand Prix car. Sports cars were a different matter, and if anything prevented Fangio from being the 'perfect' racing driver it was his dislike for this type of

Juan Fangio – Superstar. Drifting through Aintree's Melling Crossing ess-bend in the W196 Mercedes during the 1955 British Grand Prix

Swansong — Fangio's *Piccolo* Maserati howls past the Reims pits in company with Harry Schell's BRM during the five-times World Champion's last race — the 1958 French GP. It was ten years after his European debut . . . also at Reims

racing. Moss could outperform The Old Man in the Mercedes-Benz 300SLR during 1955, but it was not a true measure of respective ability. Fangio in his greatest European years just did not turn on in this kind of car — he did not always 'try'.

He had come into top-class racing as a fully mature man; indeed at an age when some others are retiring, and his impassive ability to judge the necessary speed at which he could win a race was a mark of such maturity.

He was always fit, had incredible stamina and machine-like concentration when racing, and to these attributes he added an uncanny 'feel' for a sick car — nursing many to the finish line when other drivers would have thrown in the towel or butchered the car completely.

Fangio was always an undemonstrative man, unexcitable to the point of stoicism, and even when roused to drive a car beyond its normally-accepted limits he still looked relaxed

and calm within its cockpit.

A man of sober habits, he spent his 20-year racing life travelling with one woman, Andreina, kept a frugal diet, swore by 12 hours sleep each night and preferred mineral water to wine. He spoke his native Spanish and a little Italian in a curiously high, piping voice, and after his Monza crash held his head stiffly, turning his whole body to look round with his steel-blue eyes.

Since his retirement he has built up a motor trading empire in his native Argentine, where of course he is a national hero, and he still keeps in touch with the racing world. Even today when his sober-suited form appears at a race meeting he is immediately recognised, and the flood of autograph hunters is a mark of his reputation, for most of them can never have seen him race.

Juan Fangio was simply the best driver of his day, and his achievements are still the first target at which today's young lions must aim . . .

Jim Clark

Jimmy Clark was the driver who succeeded Fangio in setting the standard of his time and combining that talent with World Championship success. Stirling Moss, whose mantle he assumed in 1962, had taken Fangio's place four years previously but events had always combined to cheat him of that prestigious title. As Clark's talents developed in the early 1960s, Moss judged the likable, uncomplicated Scot to be 'the only man I fear . . .'

Jim Clark was the son of a well-to-do Scottish sheep farmer. In 1942 the family moved to Duns, in the border country of Berwickshire, and took over the 1240-acre Edington Mains farm where Jimmy grew up. There he had his earliest experience of driving, playing around the tractors and steering his father's Austin Seven around the farm lanes at the age of nine.

An Alvis Speed Twenty was revived in 1946, and the boy was allowed to drive around the farm; two years later Jimmy had his first contact with somebody involved in motor racing. This was Alec Calder, a local farmer whom Jimmy's eldest sister Mattie married that year. He had a 3-litre Bentley and a Brooklands Riley. In the school holidays Jimmy was staying with relatives down in Kent when he was taken to a race meeting at the new Brands Hatch track. He found the whole thing very exciting, and bought an autographed picture of a new young driver, named Stirling Moss.

Jimmy was schooled at Clifton Hall in Edinburgh, and at Loretto, the public school. He was no great scholar, but a good sportsman, playing cricket, rugby and hockey.

The airfield circuit of Winfield was only about six miles from Edington Mains, but he was more interested in cricket, although as he later wrote; '. . . racing seemed to pursue me. One night I was coming back from a cricket match . . . when suddenly I met three Ecurie Ecosse C-Type Jaguars. I remember thinking what a shower of madmen they were. But at the same time I felt a slight twinge of envy . . .'

The first race meeting he saw in Scotland was at Charterhall airfield where the great Farina drove the fearsome Thin Wall Special Ferrari, and Stirling Moss was beaten by Ian Stewart's Ecurie Ecosse Jaguar.

Clark left school in 1952. His grandfather and uncle had died within two weeks of each other, and the family now had three farms to run. His future seemed mapped out, but on his 17th

Jimmy Clark at Solitude in the 1960 Lotus 18 Formula Junior-cum-2-cum-1 car in which he made his name, and began his legendarily successful nine-season career with Colin Chapman's team

Clark's face registers amazed delight as he hears from Spa's PA system that he has won the 1964 Belgian GP! In fourth place after a late-race pit stop the cars ahead of him ran out of fuel and he unwittingly pipped McLaren's spluttering Cooper to win on the line. Out at Stavelot corner on the cooling-off lap his own Lotus ran dry

Clark takes a jubilant Chapman on a lap of honour after winning at Monza in 1963 to clinch their first world title

birthday he collected a provisional driving licence, and within six weeks had passed his test and took over his father's old Sunbeam-Talbot.

He wanted to try competitive driving, and Jock McBain (a local garage owner) persuaded him to enter a Berwick and District Motor Club driving tests meeting at nearby Winfield. The results showed him winning, but as he was not a club member he never gained an award. Thereafter a string of minor rallies and driving tests followed.

In June, 1956, Jimmy Clark had his first race, driving his friend Ian Scott-Watson's DKW *Sonderklasse* at Crimond. He finished eighth. As the season progressed the amiable young farmer scored several class victories in his own ageing Sunbeam and in the 'Deek', and for 1957 Scott-Watson invested in a Porsche 1600 Super which had belonged to motor racing band leader, Billy Cotton. His performances in that car fired Clark's enthusiasm once and for all . . . counselled, pushed, guided and cajoled the whole time by Ian Scott-Watson.

The 1958 season found the future World Champion beginning to go motor racing seriously. As he was the only son of the family (he had four elder sisters) his parents tried to dissuade him, but they could not staunch his growing enthusiasm.

Jock McBain and some friends reformed the Border Reivers team — named after the old marauding gangs of the border country — and they asked Clark to drive their newly-acquired, and reputedly ex-Archie Scott-Brown, D-Type Jaguar.

He ended the season with 12 wins from 20 starts, and was eighth in a macabre Continental debut in the *Coupe de Spa*, in which he witnessed the popular, one-handed Scott-Brown's fiery fatal accident.

Late that year Scott-Watson bought a Lotus Elite, and Clark raced it at Brands Hatch against Lotus boss Colin Chapman, collided with a back marker, and lost a great race. Chapman had already been impressed by the Scot's ability in a test drive of the new Formula 2 Lotus at Brands Hatch, but in 1959 his admiration grew as Clark really made his name in the Reivers' Lister-Jaguar. He won twelve races, and shared a semi-works Lotus Elite with Sir John Whitmore at Le Mans,

to place second in class in the 24-Hours classic.

On December 26, 1959, Jim Clark had his first single-seater race, a depressing outing in a front-engined Formula Junior Gemini on a damp track at Brands Hatch. That same Boxing Day meeting saw him suffer his first racing accident, as he spun Scott-Watson's Elite into the bank.

Meanwhile Reg Parnell, who knew McBain, gave Jimmy an Aston Martin driver trial and signed-him on for their Formula 1 team. Luckily for Clark, the front-engined Astons were delayed, and he was released from his contract, and joined Team Lotus to drive Formula 2 and Formula Junior cars.

The rear-engined Lotus 18 set new performance standards in those classes in 1960, and Jim's first season with Team Lotus yielded nine wins.

By the time of the Dutch Grand Prix in June, Chapman was convinced of his young protégé's potential, and Clark made his World Championship race debut there, running as high as fourth before his car's gearbox packed-up. Two weeks later he went to the Belgian Grand Prix on the daunting Spa circuit, finished fifth, scoring his first Championship points — and saw the after effects of fatal accidents to his team-mate Alan Stacey, and Cooper driver Chris Bristow.

These tragic events, following on Scott-Brown's accident on the same circuit two years previously, left Clark ever after with an intense dislike for Spa — but he was to meet its challenge fully in years to come.

By 1961 he was a permanent member of the Lotus Formula 1 team. He was only 25 but was a complete professional, totally absorbed in his work. He started his winning career in Formula 1 during this season, scoring at Pau, and in the Rand, Natal, and South African GPs at the close of the calendar. But again tragedy had marred his career, for in the Italian Grand Prix at Monza his Lotus had collided with Wolfgang von Trips' Ferrari, which ran into the crowd, killing several spectators and its German driver.

Clark's inate ability and enthusiasm kept him racing, and once in the cock-

pit his mind put these darker moments behind him, and fused man and car in a way seldom seen before, or since.

In 1962 Chapman introduced the stressed-skin monocoque Lotus 25 and Clark won his first Championship round in it — at Spa! The season developed into a running battle between

Top: Clark never won at Monaco, and here in 1967 he climbs from his 2-litre Lotus-Climax 33 after being forced down the Chicane escape road early in the race. He left it finally when the car's suspension failed

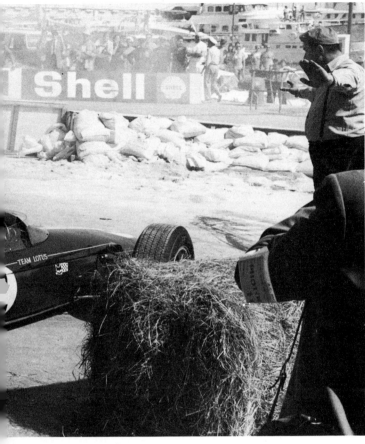

Above: as a 'Rooky' at Indianapolis in 1963 Clark was only narrowly beaten into second place in his Lotus 29. A green car was bad enough, but to have the Ford V8 engine in the rear and 'no proper chassis' was unbelievable!

drivers could live with him.

He scored a record seven *Grande Epreuve* victories in that 1963 chase for the Championship, four of them consecutively, and earned the World Championship crown he so richly deserved. At 27, he was the youngest Champion yet.

That unique year also saw his debut at Indianapolis for the 500-mile race, and he shook the American track racing establishment by finishing a challenging second in a rear-engined Lotus-Ford which they saw as a joke.

Jim Clark was *the* star driver of the time, but despite all the publicity and the glamorous aura surrounding him, he remained the modest, quietly-spoken Border farmer; uncomfortable yet capable in the limelight, unassuming, and friendly out of it.

He was an inquisitive driver, anxious to know what other cars were like to drive, and what other kinds of racing were about. He appeared in large and small saloons, in sports cars and even in American NASCAR racing with their huge, brutish stock cars. In some cases these were once-only drives, and he did not repeat the experiment, having satisfied himself that he now knew what racing a Galaxie or a NASCAR stocker was all about. A major feature of British meetings at this time was the sight of Clark three-wheeling a works Lotus-Cortina in saloon car supporting events, or fisting a potent yet fragile Lotus 30 sports car around on a knife-edge of control.

The only road racing class he did not tackle seriously was long-distance sports car racing, after early forays at Le Mans and the Nürburgring. Like Fangio this was an omission which was to win him some minor criticism. Like Fangio there is no doubt he could have been as good in a soapbox as he was in a GP car but he did not prove it. Like Fangio it left a tiny chink in his armour-plated reputation.

The $1\frac{1}{2}$-litre Formula 1 cars of the time were largely unspectacular. Their characteristics prevented Clark being as exciting to watch as Fangio or any of the earlier aces in their front-engined cars, yet his unflurried style and complete, cool concentration were from

Jimmy and Graham Hill's BRM, which was not resolved until the final round in South Africa when Clark's Lotus failed after establishing a commanding lead. He had won the British and United States Grands Prix, plus five non-Championship Formula 1 races, and in the following season no other

45

the same mould. In saloon and sports cars, or in the bigger-engined categories, Jim Clark was visibly the master at work.

In 1965 he regained the World Championship title, won Indianapolis at his third attempt and then went into the new 3-litre Grand Prix Formula in 1966 with a basically obsolete car – a 2-litre Lotus-Climax – while full 3-litre BRM H16-engined Lotuses were being prepared. He fought against great odds all season, and was lucky to escape serious harm when a bird hit him in the face in practice at Reims. At Watkins Glen for the United States Grand Prix his luck changed, and while faster runners hit trouble he nursed his ailing Lotus-BRM home in first place.

In 1967 the new Lotus 49 with its Cosworth-Ford V8 engine made its debut in the Dutch Grand Prix, and there Clark gave it a fairy-tale baptism by winning the race at record speed. He ran Hulme very close for the Championship, winning his *fifth* British Grand Prix, and his third United States and Mexican races. He was always the man to watch, and the man to beat, and with the potent new Lotus rapidly reaching full development 1968 should have been another Clark year.

But he had his problems. The British tax system weighed heavily on him, for he had become one of the first really big money-earners in motor racing. He took up residence in Paris, rarely appearing in the UK apart from such major events as the British Grand Prix. Edington Mains was still his farm, and it was managed for him, but the pressures were beginning to tell. He kept his growing unhappiness well under control, but its sad story was told in every line on his suddenly ageing face.

At the beginning of 1968 he won the South African Grand Prix to score his 25th Championship-qualifying victory, breaking Fangio's ten-year old record of 24. He then completed a tour of Australia and New Zealand, to win his second Tasman Championship, and then returned expectantly to Europe.

On April 7, 1968, Jim Clark was racing his uncompetitive Lotus 48 in the opening round of the European F2 Championship at Hockenheim, in Germany. He was lying eighth on the fifth lap of the first heat, finding the going very difficult with wide tyres on a wet track.

He seemed to be in some engine trouble, and had waved two cars past on the previous lap when the Lotus slid off the right-handed Shrimp Curve on the back of the course. It broadsided

Clark's wheel-waving antics with the works Lotus-Cortinas delighted British crowds at those much-lamented non-Championship Formula 1 meetings in which the top drivers would also drive saloon, sports and GT cars during the day's programme. Here the Scot obliges at Aintree

through some saplings, and then there had to be a stouter tree in its path. It smashed into that tree with terrific force, catching the trunk full in the cockpit and breaking in two.

Jimmy was picked-up with massive head and thoracic injuries, and was already beyond help when taken to Heidelberg Hospital. The wreckage was so badly mangled it gave little clue to the cause of the accident, but the most probable explanation was that the right rear tyre lost pressure, and left the rim when thrown-out at high speed, putting the car into an immediate broadside beyond human control.

But Jim Clark had been killed, and to all who knew him it was simply unbelievable; to many it is unbelievable still. He had been a complete natural, capable of adapting himself to any conditions, whether wet or dry, oily or windy, and to any car. He was simply *too good* to have been killed. . .

His lap times were always indicative of a car's optimum performance, whatever its trim or state of preparation, and he *never* had an off day. Several times he experienced mechanical failures which could easily have been fatal to a lesser man, but his special qualities of reflex and car control kept him out of trouble.

While he won on super-fast circuits like Spa and Monza, he did equally well around the houses at Pau, and was the quickest man around Monaco although he never finished there. Like all great sportsmen he shone in adversity, and as early as 1962 he had turned in a great David and Goliath performance in the Nürburgring 1000 Kilometre race, when he led for many laps in a tiny Lotus 23 sports car until a combination of failing brakes and exhaust fumes in the cockpit put him off into the bushes. Then again he put all his dislike and misgivings about the Spa circuit to one side, and drove well enough to win four consecutive Belgian Grands Prix there, although admittedly with Lady Luck very much on his side.

But finally she deserted this gifted, intensely popular 'Flying Scotsman' — the enthusiastic schoolboy who had never grown cynical or over-professional — and Jimmy died in a Lotus cockpit. In many ways the racing world never recovered from his loss. . .

Stewart playing 'Trilby' to Ken Tyrrell's Svengali in the Clermont paddock. There was no cleverer combination in Grand Prix racing from 1969 to 1973

John Young 'Jackie' Stewart
BORN JUNE 11, 1939, DUMBARTON, SCOTLAND

Whenever a great driver has faded from the scene, or has been wrenched from it so tragically as was Jim Clark, there has always been another standing in the wings ready to take his place. Jackie Stewart was just such a driver, and he set the standard from 1968 to his retirement in 1973.

He set a record of 27 World Championship Grand Prix race wins in his career, and amassed a record total of 360 Championship points. He was also the biggest money-earner ever on the Grand Prix scene; his vociferous safety campaigning helped change the face of motor racing; he took a lot out of the sport; he put a very great deal into it. . .

Jackie Stewart was the younger son of Dumbarton's Jaguar dealer, whose Dumbuck Garage was a small but prosperous business with a reputation for high-quality work. Elder brother Jimmy Stewart drove for Ecurie Ecosse and Aston Martin in the mid-1950s but had retired in deference to maternal wishes following a crash at Le Mans.

At that time 15-year-old Jackie was working as a mechanic at Dumbuck. He had watched some of Jimmy's racing, but with encouragement from his father had turned to trap shooting instead. He was good, very good . . . and was representing Scotland in his mid-'teens. In 1959 and 1960 he won the British, Irish, Scottish, Welsh and English Championships, and the *Grand Prix des Nations*.

He was an intensely competitive young man, with a terrific, inborn will to succeed. In 1960, on his 21st birthday, he failed dismally while shooting for selection to the British Olympic team and it hurt desperately.

He accepted the failure as 'experience' but his interest in shooting declined thereafter as his fascination with motor racing increased. One of the Dumbuck Garage's wealthier customers was Barry Filer, and they prepared a string of interesting cars which he owned and which he and some friends raced in club events.

The younger Stewart accompanied Filer's cars as mechanic, and began driving occasionally in Filer's Marcos GT, Aston Martin DB4GT, an AC Ace and eventually in Dumbuck's own Jaguar E-Type demonstrator. He drove as 'A. N. Other' to keep the secret from his parents, but the same natural sense of timing and lightning reflexes which had made him such a good shot now made his driving simply too good to be kept secret.

Early in 1962 his supporters arranged a private test session at Oulton Park, in which Jackie's times were so good that he decided to tackle motor racing seriously. One of his mentors was top-ranking Scots motorcycle ace Bob McIntyre, and his death in a racing accident in August that year was felt keenly by young Stewart. Perhaps it made him even more fiercely determined to succeed.

Ecurie Ecosse, now long past their former glories, gave him some drives in an ancient Cooper Monaco, and in

one race at Goodwood he impressed track manager Robin McKay so much that McKay mentioned the young Scot's budding prowess to Ken Tyrrell.

He was a former racing driver who had run Cooper Formula 2, Junior and saloon car teams from his timber yard business in Surrey. Tough, experienced, uncompromising Tyrrell knew Jimmy Stewart, and he asked him how serious were Jackie's ambitions. When he learned that the younger brother was deadly serious he invited him to Goodwood to test drive the new Formula 3 Cooper-BMC. Cooper works driver Bruce McLaren set a base time, Jackie equalled and then bettered it, and Tyrrell signed him on the spot.

From this point forward, Stewart's career was made. In 1964 he won every Formula 3 race he entered, except two. By mid-summer he had finished second to Denny Hulme in his first Formula 2 drive – in a works Ron Harris-entered Lotus at Clermont-Ferrand and had sampled Jimmy Clark's Formula 1 Lotus in practice for the British Grand Prix at Brands Hatch (he spun it!). In September he won for the Ron Harris Formula 2 Lotus team at Snetterton, and at the end of the year he deputised for Jimmy Clark (who had slipped a disc) in the Formula 1 Rand Grand Prix in South Africa. He won the second heat – his first Formula 1 victory – after shearing both drive shafts in the first heat.

The Grand Prix teams fell over themselves to sign Stewart, and he put his faith in BRM, to become Graham Hill's team-mate. He was sixth in his World Championship debut race in South Africa, immediately scoring a Championship point, and back home he scored his first outright Formula 1 victory in the International Trophy race at Silverstone.

He was third at Monaco, second on his first appearance at the daunting Spa circuit – where he really proved his enormous potential – and followed with two more second places at Clermont and Zandvoort.

Everywhere he went he was tailing his compatriot and increasingly close friend Jim Clark, and his meteoric progress immediately put all other drivers

Jackie Stewart making his name in one of Ken Tyrrell's works Formula 3 Cooper-BMCs at Aintree in the 1964 '200' meeting

In 1967 BRM continued to use their 2·1-litre Tasman V8 cars while the unreliable H16 hung fire. Here Stewart takes his Tasman Championship-winning car into third place in the French GP at Le Mans' Bugatti Circuit

Above: Mike Hawthorn's Super Squalo Ferrari makes a splash of red against the Barcelona straw bales on its way to victory in the 1954 Spanish Grand Prix at Pedralbes

Left: Juan Manuel Fangio was less than content during his 1956 season with Ferrari, but he still clinched his fourth World Championship title in their ill-handling Lancia-derived V8 cars. Here he is on his way to his unique win in the British GP at Silverstone

Right: Phil Hill, the only American driver ever to win the World Championship, pictured at Zandvoort with the 1962 Ferrari Dino 156

— except Clark — in the shade. A win had to come, and in the Italian Grand Prix at Monza he led his BRM team leader, Graham Hill, out of the last bend and across the line to clinch it.

This 1965 season ended with J. Y. Stewart third in the World Championship behind Clark and Hill, and during a winter tour of Australia and New Zealand the jaunty, effervescent young man from the Clyde Valley won the Tasman Championship for BRM.

In May he appeared in a Mecom Lola at Indianapolis and led the freakish, accident-marred race for many laps until an engine oil scavenge pump failed. This performance, and his apparently carefree, jaunty walk back to the pits from the abandoned Lola,

immediately endeared him to American fans accustomed to histrionics.

Then came the Belgian Grand Prix, at Spa, and on the first lap the field ran into a freak cloudburst. Stewart's Tasman BRM aquaplaned and spun through railings down into a sunken garden in Masta Hamlet. He was trapped semi-conscious, soaked in petrol from ruptured tanks, until Graham Hill and Bob Bondurant — whose BRMs had crashed nearby — came to his aid. They winkled him out of the wreckage with a broken shoulder, cracked rib and fuel burns, and it was ages before the ambulance arrived to take him to hospital. This traumatic experience set back Stewart's full development by two

First World Championship for Stewart came in 1969 driving the Tyrrell-managed Matra-Cosworths. A feature of the season was the rivalry between Jackie and his friend Jochen Rindt. Here in the British GP at Silverstone they run 1–2, Matra leading Lotus

Following pages: the dominant partnership of the 1960s — Jim Clark and Lotus-Climax — dives into Thillois Hairpin at Reims on the way to victory in the 1963 French GP, one of their record seven Championship-qualifying wins in a season

years, gave him the kind of mental block about Spa which Clark had escaped, and hardened his determination to improve racing safety.

As BRM went into sad decline to the end of 1967, so Stewart struggled with their difficult H16 cars and gave them better results than they perhaps deserved. Meanwhile he stayed with the Tyrrell team in Formula 2, as he had with their Cooper cars in 1965 and then with their increasingly-promising Matras in 1966–67. As he regained his full confidence following the Spa crash and Tyrrell's team sorted-out their Matra-Cosworths, Stewart began winning once more — at Albi, Oulton Park, Enna and Karlskoga late in 1967.

Ken had been to the Dutch Grand Prix that year, and had witnessed Jim Clark's victorious debut with the new Cosworth-Ford V8-powered Lotus 49. These engines were to be offered for general sale in 1968 and Tyrrell placed an immediate order, and then began beating the bushes for a suitable chassis, and talking to Stewart as a suitable driver.

With backing from the newly-formed French ELF oil consortium and from Dunlop tyres, Tyrrell was able to afford Stewart's personal faith in him, and the Scot rejected offers from Ferrari among other teams to join Ken's new Equipe Matra International, using developed chassis from the French aerospace company.

The new team's debut was in South Africa, where Jimmy Clark won his record-breaking 25th and last Grand Prix and Stewart's Matra-Ford led the opening lap. The year could well have been a vintage season with Stewart versus Clark, but it was not to be, as Jimmy's death hit his countryman hard . . . and low.

Then in a Formula 2 race at Jarama in Spain, Stewart crashed mildly but broke the tiny scaphoid bone in his right wrist. The injury kept him out of the Spanish and Monaco Grands Prix, and the Indy '500'

He reappeared at Spa, driving with his wrist in a plastic cast, conquered his dislike of the open road course and would have won but for an uncharacteristic Tyrrell lapse which allowed the Matra to run out of fuel, on the penultimate lap. He won the Dutch Grand Prix in the wet, exhausted himself totally in wrestling the Matra around Brands Hatch to take sixth place, and in Germany he drove probably the race of his life, bravely, superbly, to win a mist-shrouded, rain-soaked Grand Prix on the Nürburgring by no less than a *four-minute* margin!

He was exhausted as he finished, and had the weather been dry and wide dry-weather tyres been fitted to the Matra it is doubtful if his wrist could have stood the pace. As it was, the narrower wet-weather tyres lightened the steering and made a classical, intensely worthy drive possible.

At Watkins Glen he won the United States Grand Prix to increase his vast American following, and he was in the running to take the Championship in the final round in Mexico when a fuel blockage ruined his chances.

In 1969 the story improved. Stewart and the new Matra-Ford were virtually unbeatable, winning six Grand Prix races to secure their first, long-expected World Championship titles. He wanted very much to equal Clark's seven-in-a-season record but it was not to be.

For 1970 Tyrrell adopted March chassis to stay with the Ford engine, while Matra concentrated on their own V12, and despite the new marque's shortcomings Stewart drove well enough to have retained his title but for a spate of engine failures. He won only the Spanish Grand Prix, and by the North American races at the close of the year he was driving a brand-new Tyrrell car, leading in Canada and America to give notice for 1971.

That season saw Stewart consistently second to the 12-cylinder Ferraris in the early races, and then pulling a superb drive out of the bag in an indifferently set-up car to win at Barcelona. This victory set the pattern for the rest of the season as he won at Monaco (another classic drive, with his Tyrrell's rear brakes inoperative), in France, Britain, Germany and Canada. At Silverstone the scrutineers paid Tyrrell and Stewart the signal honour of carefully checking the win-

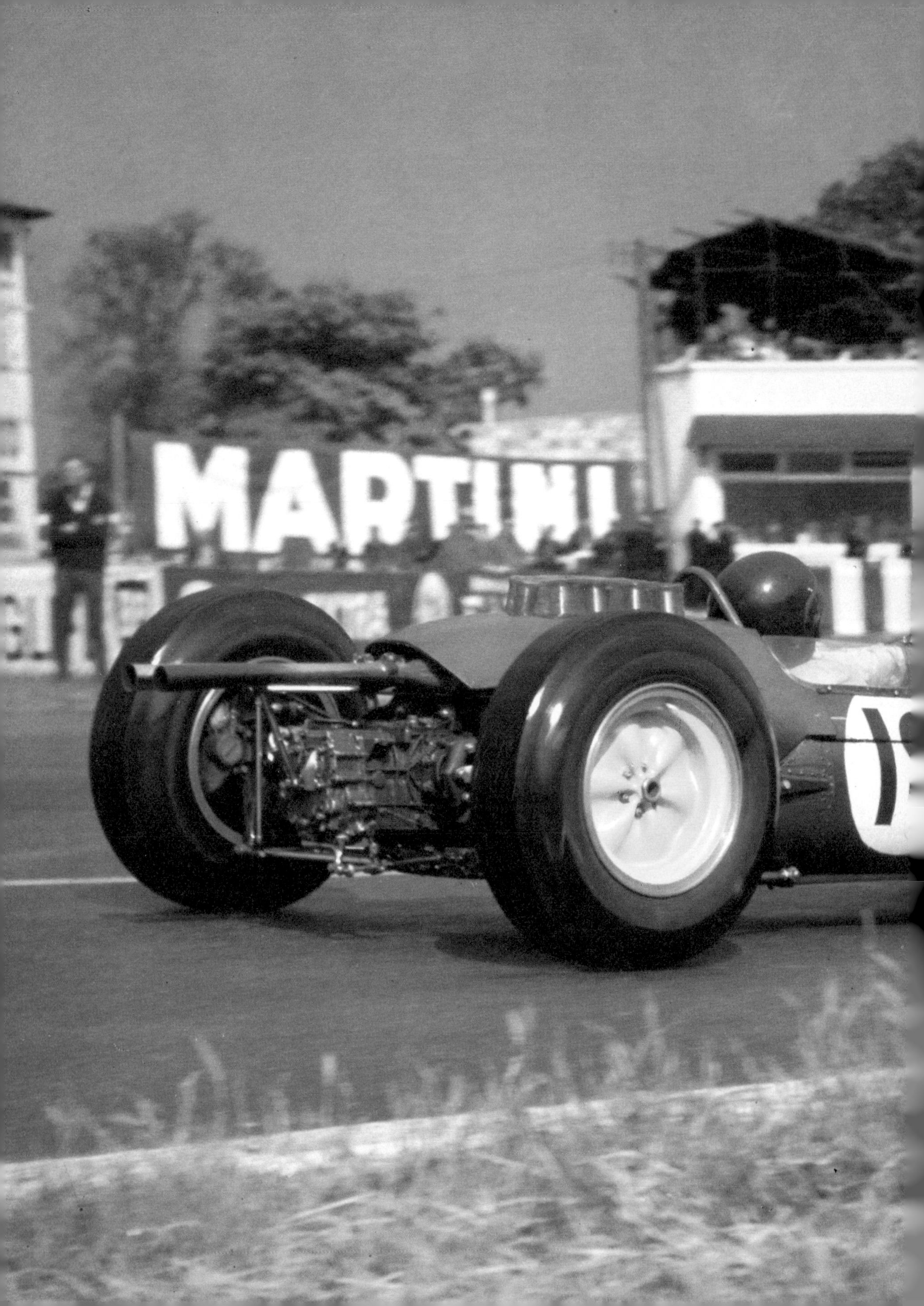
MARTINI

ning engine's capacity, while in France the car's ELF fuel had been analysed from a sample thoughtfully tapped-off at the pressure gauge! Yes, the combination of Stewart and Tyrrell and Cosworth really were that good. . .

It was in the pits at the Osterreichring that Stewart discovered he was World Champion for the second time. His car was abandoned out on the circuit after losing a wheel, but Jacky Ickx — his only rival — had also retired his Ferrari.

The 1972 season was more fraught, and for the first time Tyrrell found his ace driver having off days. A stomach ulcer was diagnosed, the dynamic, promotion-minded Scot relaxed his jet-set executive programme, and missed two Grands Prix. When he returned he had a lucky win in France to add to his season-opening victory in South Africa, but not until the new-look Tyrrells reached full development for the North American races did he win again. Emerson Fittipaldi journeyed to Canada and America as reigning champion, but Stewart won both races to prove who was best before what had become virtually his crowd.

He was runner-up in the World Championship, and he went into 1973 knowing that he was going to retire at its end, and that he wanted to retire on top. He did just that, all his experienced racecraft compensating for the increasing speed of Ronnie Peterson and the tactical pace of Fittipaldi in the works Lotuses.

With wins in South Africa and Belgium, Stewart equalled Clark's long-standing record of 25 *Grande Epreuve* victories at Monaco. Then in Holland and Germany he added two more to set a new standard of 27 Championship-qualifying race wins.

At Monza he lost over one minute in the pits, while a punctured wheel was changed. He rejoined in 20th place, and *tigered*. After 14 laps he was eighth. Two laps later he was seventh with a new record lap to his credit. Then he gobbled-up Ickx's Ferrari, then Hailwood, then Reutemann. He was fifth behind his teammate, Francois Cevert, who waved him through into fourth place — and its

three Championship points — in which he finished. It was his last race in Europe; '*What* a drive . . .' growled the normally *blasé* Ken Tyrrell; it clinched Jackie Stewart's third World title.

In Canada he disgraced himself by forgetting team orders in a rain-marred race, and coming in to change tyres too soon, and then the American Grand Prix at Watkins Glen was to be his one hundredth and last World Championship race. In practice, his team-mate Cevert died in a ghastly accident. Jackie practised his car half-heartedly after the calamity, and ELF Team Tyrrell then withdrew from the race. The three-time World Champion, standard-setter of his time, had become an ex-racing driver. . .

In many ways Jackie Stewart was dogged by such tragedy. He was affected by Bob McIntyre's death at the dawn of his career. Jim Clark's death took much of the gilt from his 1968 season in which he won three Grands Prix and nearly took the Championship. In 1970 Bruce McLaren was killed, a man whom Stewart respected greatly, and then his close friends Piers Courage and Jochen Rindt had both died in Grand Prix accidents.

After taking his second title in 1971, a celebratory Formula 1 race was held in his honour at Brands Hatch. It was stopped when Jo Siffert's BRM crashed and exploded into a fatal fireball before the new Champion's eyes. . . . When he broke Jimmy Clark's record of 25 *Grande Epreuve* victories by winning his 26th at Zandvoort he drove lap after lap past the harrowing, sheet-shrouded wreck of Roger Williamson's burned-out March. Then his successful farewell season in 1973 had to end on such a harrowing note.

To many, Stewart's outspoken, insistent, and extremely influential views on his chosen sport were anathema, but with his experiences the affect on such an extrovert, confident and articulate professional are understandable.

If Stirling Moss was the first truly professional British racing driver, Jackie Stewart was his 'superstar' successor. His increasingly modish image, his jet-set life style, his supreme promotional talents, vectored care-

Beady eyes glinting through his visor, Jackie Stewart awaits to rejoin the 1973 British GP after an excursion through the cornfield at Stowe corner. It was a rare lapse in his third and final World Championship-winning season. The car is Tyrrell 006/2

Following pages: a gridful of talent prepares for the 1966 British Grand Prix at Brands Hatch; Brabham, Hulme and Gurney on the front row ahead of Graham Hill and Clark, with Surtees, Rindt and Stewart behind them — seven World Champions

fully into big money markets by the Mark McCormack organisation which handled many other sporting super-stars, were all parts of a marketable and well marketed package.

He was not a man who would squander his talents for any personal enthusiasm, as would Jim Clark who drove anything just for the fun of it, and his 1971 season for example consisted purely of the 11 Championship Grand Prix races, and none other. To many this was modern 'professionalism' at its worst.

He spent the rest of his time testing, practising and testing again, then in between times selling himself, and more important, selling his sport, to

millions of people across the World. If the sport which they see now is rather different from the sport some enthusiasts remember with affection — perhaps it is thanks to media men such as this self-made Swiss-domiciled Scot that it survives at all.

Today Jackie Stewart still jet-sets around the World, talking motor cars and motor racing, promoting, backing, selling as never before. He has proved himself an excellent TV race commentator in Britain and America, and lives at Begnins, above Lake Geneva, with his wife Helen and their two young sons. Jackie Stewart is making sure he will not be forgotten. He could well relax . . . his exploits are unforgettable.

The Uncrowned Champions

Stirling Moss and Ronnie Peterson have quite a lot in common. Both began their competition careers in their teens; Moss never won the World Championship; Peterson has not won it yet. It is a title which both deserved, and which both wanted desperately.

The top accolade in any sport does not necessarily fall to the best man around, unless he has good fortune to match his pace-setting ability. Both Stirling Moss and Ronnie Peterson have been the pace-setters of their time, and uncrowned Champions . . .

Stirling Crauford Moss

BORN SEPTEMBER 17, 1929, LONDON, ENGLAND

He was the greatest English racing driver. Sir Henry Segrave probably achieved greater fame in the rarefied atmosphere of the 1920s, but by any yardstick Stirling Moss did more for British motor racing as such than any other Englishman.

He was born into motor racing. His father, Alfred, had raced Crouch cars at Brooklands and a Fronty-Ford at Indianapolis in the 1920s, and his mother Aileen was an expert trials driver in the 1930s.

'Pa' Moss was in dentistry, but his son grew up surrounded by quality motor cars, and sharpened his taste for competition — on horseback. He badgered his parents into giving him a car as soon as he was old enough to drive it legally, and at 17 he made his debut in the Eastbourne Rally and then competed in the Brighton Speed Trials, in a 1939 BMW 328 sports car. He did not impress.

For his 18th birthday, young Stirling was given one of the new 500 cc motor-cycle-engined Cooper-JAPs by his father. The family trailed it around in a horsebox to minor sprint and hill-climb meetings during that 1948 season, and 'S. C. Moss' ended the year with ten class wins to his name, and had been blooded in circuit racing

at Goodwood and Silverstone.

Even at this early stage it was obvious that the tousle-haired youngster was someone very special. He had been thrown into the deep end of 500 cc racing, and had begun to swim immediately. He was driving in races before his techniques had been dulled by the restrictions of the public road, and was growing up purely and simply as a 'Racing Driver'.

In 1949 Cooper adopted a 998 cc

The Boy and The Old Man prepare to do battle for Mercedes-Benz in the 1955 Dutch Grand Prix at Zandvoort. Stirling Moss (left) and Juan Fangio were without doubt the greatest racing drivers of the 1950s — in the same team they dominated the sport

Name-making — Stirling Moss in the 500 cc Formula 3 Cooper. He raced on in this class for several years after becoming Britain's first motor racing 'Superstar', driving anything, anywhere, because he was a true professional who never forgot that he enjoyed his work

twin-cylinder JAP engine to allow their cars to run in Formula 2 events against conventional front-engined 2-litre cars. The little Cooper 'thousands' had a comparable power to weight ratio which made them competitive on tight circuits with a good driver on board, and Stirling Moss, at 19, was just such a driver.

On his first European tour he led a Ferrari for miles on the Garda Circuit before finishing third behind Villoresi and Tadini in a pair of the Italian cars, and the Italian press raved about the youngster in his funny English car.

They had latched onto Moss' potential long before the national media back home began their superb promotional job which made 'Stirling Moss' a household name in the early 1950s. He had ended the 1949 season with seven victories, including his first on foreign soil in a 500 cc race at Zandvoort, and in 1950 this bouncy, supremely enthusiastic 20-year-old hit the British headlines by winning the Tourist Trophy at Dundrod in a Jaguar XK120, beating the works cars. He drove Formula 2 HWMs for John Heath and George Abecassis, and harried the Ferraris on Rome's Baths of Caracalla circuit to set fastest lap. Then he was third behind the Grand

Prix Alfa Romeos of Farina and Fangio at Bari, and climbed even higher in the Italians' estimation.

Moss was a very patriotic young man, who delighted in bearding the Continentals in a normally uncompetitive British car, and at the close of that season he thoroughly deserved the first of his ten British Racing Drivers' Club Gold Star awards.

HWM gave him his Championship Grand Prix debut at Berne in 1951, where he finished eighth, but not until 1953 did he finish another *Grande Epreuve*, when his Connaught was ninth in Holland. A specially-built Cooper-Alta proved troublesome, but held together to yield sixth place in the German Grand Prix that season. Obviously there was no British car capable of doing him justice in Grand Prix racing. Mike Hawthorn had realised that and had joined Ferrari, to win the French Grand Prix for them that season, and his place in the Italian team could easily have been Moss'. Instead, his determination to succeed in a British car had made him reject a Ferrari offer.

Jaguar had given him a worthy car in sports car races in these years, in which he led at Le Mans for nine hours and set a new record lap in 1951, and

Stirling Moss, trying
typically hard to
please the crowd
after a lengthy
pit stop had dropped
him out of conten-
tion for the race lead,
at Goodwood on
Easter Monday, 1962
Seconds later his
UDT-Laystall Lotus-
Climax crashed at St
Mary's, and the
uncrowned
Champion's career
was ended.

Right: Dan Gurney and A. J. Foyt made it an all-American win at Le Mans in 1967 driving this colourful Ford Mark IV. For the Californian road-racer and the Texan track star it was an unlikely but successful partnership

then took second place there in 1953. His Sunbeam Talbot rally car brought him a coveted *Coupe des Alpes en Or* for three penalty-free 'Alpines', but his insistence on driving British in Grand Prix racing was perhaps the first of the miscalculations which held Moss and the World Championship apart.

By 1954, Stirling Moss Ltd had been formed to publicise, promote and manage this determined, totally dedicated and by this time utterly professional young man. He had become more than a racing motorist. He was a national celebrity, but he had still not proved himself as a Grand Prix driver. Alfred Neubaurer, manager of the revived Mercedes-Benz team, pointed out this failing when Moss' manager Ken Gregory offered the German team his services. Neubauer suggested that Moss stop fooling around with worthless English cars, and show his true potential in a Maserati 250F — a car which was generally competitive, and which the Italian company was only too willing to supply to private entrants.

So Moss at last set aside his misguided (though laudable) patriotism, and bought a Maserati for 1954. He was third in his first Championship race with the car, in Belgium, and by mid-season was taken under Maserati's wing, using factory engines and shining brightly despite little in the way of concrete Grand Prix results. When he led the Mercedes and Ferraris at Monza, he had arrived.

For 1955, Neubauer's reservations were set aside, and Maserati were mortified to see the young Englishman going to Mercedes for a large sum of Deutschmarks. There he found himself driving as number two to Juan Fangio, and he followed in the maestro's footsteps all season to finish runner-up in the World Championship. Fangio stepped aside at Aintree to allow Moss to become the first Englishman ever to win the British Grand Prix. Whereas the Argentinian had no taste for sports car racing, Moss revelled in it, and won the Mille Miglia, Tourist Trophy and Targa Florio to give Mercedes the World Sports Car Championship.

Moss shared this works Sunbeam with John Cutts to win one of the very rare and much-coveted Coupes d'Or for completing three consecutive International Alpine Rallies without loss of marks. The year was 1954, the place the Stelvio pass

With both major International competitions to their name, the German company withdrew from racing late that year, and in 1956 Moss rejoined Maserati's works team as number one. The Italians were so proud of him that they wore his presence like a badge. He won the Monaco and Italian Grands Prix for them, plus a string of non-Championship races, and was again runner-up to Fangio in the Championship.

Early that season he had a one-off drive for Vanwall, in the International Trophy race at Silverstone. It marked the debut of their revised, teardrop-shaped car, and Moss gave it a splendid win. Later that year, as he fulfilled his Maserati contract, he had a test day at Silverstone to decide if he should return to a British car for 1957.

What followed was typical of Moss, for he climbed from Vanwall to Connaught to BRM and back to Vanwall, doing five or six very fast laps in each with no apparent need to play himself in or acclimatise himself to these three very different motor cars. Eventually he

decided that the Vanwall was now a worthy car, and team patron Tony Vandervell — who had long been convinced that he had potentially the best car, and therefore must have the best driver — signed him on for what was at that time a small fortune in retaining fees.

By this time Moss was the complete 'Mr Motor Racing' to his own countrymen and to much of Europe, America and Australasia. As in every one of his racing seasons he appeared in all kinds of sports and touring car races, in Formula 2, in all kinds of promotional and personal appearances, and was out racing every weekend.

He was totally dedicated to his profession, and supplemented his race earnings by all kinds of peripheral activities. He was a tireless worker, with boundless dynamism, and although up late in the mornings he would keep going far into the night, without forgetting his limit when he reached it. Then he would snap off like a light, and sleep deeply, recharging his batteries for another day packed

While Fangio may have had a slight edge in the Grand Prix Mercedes, Moss made sports car racing his own with the German cars in 1955. Here he is on his way to winning the RAC Tourist Trophy at Dundrod, after a blown rear tyre had blasted the 300SLR's bodywork

with money-earning energy.

He was a keep-fit enthusiast, an accomplished water-skiier and swimmer, an intensely active, small, compact, vivid man. A liver complaint had made him unfit for National Service, but from choice he smoked seldom and drank little — it could affect his driving performance, and that was his life. What set him apart from those who followed was his visible enjoyment of his own skills. It was not all money-making. He revelled in *racing* and *raced* just whenever and wherever he could — including the public road!

In 1957 and 1958 Moss became master of the Grand Prix World in his green Vanwalls, and for them he won the British Grand Prix (sharing the first all-British win in this event with Tony Brooks), and the Pescara and Italian Grands Prix. In 1958 he added the Dutch, Portuguese and Moroccan Grands Prix to his tally in the Vanwall, while in the Argentine race — which Vanwall did not attend — he scored a classic victory in Rob Walker's experimental 2-litre mid-engined Cooper-Climax. He nursed the car to the finish with its tyres worn through to the canvas . . .

Both these seasons saw him runner-up yet again to the World Champion, in 1958 being pipped to the title by just one point — by his compatriot, Mike Hawthorn, in a Ferrari. . .

Moss was always a man who needed to feel he had some technical superiority. His Vanwall contract gave him choice of cars, and he exercised that choice to the 'Nth' degree — for example picking the chassis from one of the three cars he had tried in a practice session at Monaco, and then demanding the engine from the second and the gearbox from the third.

In 1959 Rob Walker's private Cooper team acquired Moss' skills, and his peccadilloes, and this passion for technical tinkering led to his adopting a Colotti gearbox for his car which failed with monotonous regularity. He won in Portugal and Italy when the car held together, but time after time his 'innovation' failed him and cost Championship points.

Stirling Moss had all the ability to beat his opposition in an *equal* car, but his almost pathological need for some secret advantage foiled him time and again. So it was that he could do no better than third place in the 1959 points table. . .

For 1960 Rob Walker acquired one of the new Lotus 18s and an updated Cooper. Moss found that he preferred the lightweight, delicate Lotus, and he won with it at Monaco before suffering his first serious accident when the car threw a rear wheel in practice at Spa. The car somersaulted off the bank at Malmédy at well over 100 mph, pitching out its driver with both legs and his nose broken, and a vertebra crushed. But Moss was — as always — extremely fit, and he was racing again in Portugal after missing only two races. He won the United States Grand Prix at Riverside to finish this chequered season, and placed third in the Championship once more. . .

There was a new Grand Prix Formula for 1961, in which it was obvious that new British engines were going to be a long time coming. The season should have been a clear run for Ferrari, but Moss stood in their way and took his now obsolescent Lotus 18 to brilliant, against-the-odds victories on the two most arduous circuits, at Monaco and the Nürburgring. He loved the idea of the four-wheel drive Ferguson, and he took it to the system's only Formula 1 victory in the late-season non-Championship race at Oulton Park.

Third place in the title chase for the third consecutive season must have been mortifying for the man who was still the fastest and best all-round driver of his day, but in 1962 the Walker team were re-arming with Climax V8 engines and this just had to be Stirling's season — at last.

He was still only 32, but in the early-season non-Championship race at Goodwood — where he had begun his racing career — he suffered an inexplicable accident; his Lotus 18/21 just bounding straight on into the outside bank in the difficult St Mary's Essbend.

Moss had been carving his way through the field after a pit-stop, not with any hope of winning, but simply

Another sports car — this time the big Aston Martin DBR2. In 1959 Moss persuaded David Brown to allow him to run a similar car in the Nürburgring 1000 Kms, which he won. The team cars won Le Mans and Moss co-drove the winning Aston in the Goodwood TT to bring the World Championship to Britain. It was a triumph largely of Moss's making

Moss's special skills hard at work to control Rob Walker's broadsiding Lotus 18 as it leaves the Monaco chicane during the 1960 Grand Prix. Stirling gathered it up to win . . . one almost adds, of course. One year later he won again, in the same car, against the V6 Ferraris

Moss the dynamo —
preparing to charge
after a late pit stop in
the 1957 British GP,
which he and Tony
Brooks won for
Vanwall. It was
Vanwall's first World
Championship-
qualifying victory,
and the first all-
British win in the
home event

proving to the crowd, to his competitors and to himself that he was 'The Best'. Now, abruptly, he was being cut out of a tangle of smashed wreckage, and taken to hospital unconscious and critically ill.

Recovery was a slow business, and a year passed before he was well enough to try his hand in a Lotus 19 sports car back at the Goodwood circuit. He found his old sight and reflex capabilities impaired, and the drive proved to his own disgust that he could never again be the driver he had been. He could still be good, but his

old edge — his special qualities, that inborn secret advantage — had been claimed by the earth bank at St Mary's.

Unlike many great sportsmen, Moss knew when to retire, and that was the time. He could no longer be the best, and being merely good was not good enough. He was to reappear for 'fun', races in later years, but it was the end of a sparkling career; the start of a new life for the best-ever English driver.

Perhaps the true irony of his retirement was that in the light of what followed he — in time — could still perhaps have been good enough . . .

Bengt Ronald 'Ronnie' Peterson

BORN FEBRUARY 14, 1944, OREBRÖ, SWEDEN

It was beginning to look as though Ronnie Peterson was never going to win a Grand Prix. During 1973 his black-and-gold works Lotus had led Championship rounds in Spain, Monaco, Belgium and Sweden, and had failed every time.

Then came the French Grand Prix at Ricard-Castellet, and there Ronnie's bad luck deserted him to attack his team-mate, Emerson Fittipaldi, and the tall, blonde Swede took the lead he was never to lose.

After that success, in his 40th Grand Prix, he never looked back, placing second in Britain, again having his car falter while leading in Holland, winning in Austria when Fittipaldi's car failed once more, and then beating his team-mate fair and square yet somewhat controversially at Monza. He ended the season with a terrific victory in the United States Grand Prix at Watkins Glen, and to this tally of four *Grande Epreuve* successes he added a record total of nine pole position starts in the 15 Grand Prix races of the year. There was no doubting Peterson's prowess as top-class road racing's latest pace-setter, and in 1974 — when his Lotuses became virtually obsolescent — his fearless speed and tigrish style brought him three more Grand Prix victories to underline that status.

Ronnie Peterson is the son of a baker from the small Swedish town of Orebrö. Father Bengt was an enthu-

siastic amateur racing driver, part of the 500 cc Formula 3 movement which swept Sweden after the war, when he built his own car. He retired from racing when Ronnie was six, and had already caught 'The Bug'.

The Orebrö school staff were driven to distraction by wild cycle races in the yard, usually won by young Peterson, and in his teens Ronnie graduated to motor cycles and took to moto-cross and speedway riding.

Ronnie Peterson — the Swedish one-time kart racer, Stewart's successor as the standard setter of his day — but a standard setter who lost his way

He had left school at 15, with little going for him academically, worked in a garage and then became a lift installation engineer, working all over Sweden. His cat-like reflexes were proved early when he jumped out of a lift that had gone out of control. A work-mate with him was not so quick, and was badly hurt when the lift plummeted to the ground.

Peterson wanted to buy a bigger bike, but his father refused to loan him the money, saying it was better for him to wait until he was 17 and old enough to race a kart. Four wheels you see . . .

frustrating failure to put down to experience — the first of many.

Financially, the Petersons were not a wealthy family, but they were rich in enthusiasm and had a voracious capacity for hard work. While Ronnie was accepting the karting disappointment in his typically stolid, philosophical way, he and his father and a few friends were building a Formula 3 racing car for his use.

It was based on a 1965 Brabham, using a Holbay-Ford engine, but such a combination simply was not good enough for 1966. Ronnie was third in

The controversial Italian GP win in 1973 when Ronnie pipped team-mate Fittipaldi to the line and so robbed the Brazilian reigning World Champion of his last chance of retaining the title. He was to win the race again in 1974 and 1976

now that was proper racing.

So in the winter of 1961, Bengt and Ronnie Peterson built themselves a racing kart using a German Ardie engine — hence the name 'Robardie'. In Robardie karts Ronnie Peterson rocketed around the kart circuits of Europe, and in 1966 the World Championship meeting at Copenhagen was to be decided between him and the Italian girl, Suzy Raganelli.

All weekend, the Robardie had a mysterious fault. It was underpowered, and engine changes made no improvement. What the father and son team had forgotten to change was the carburettor, which was defective, and so the Championship went to Miss Raganelli while the Petersons had a

it in his first race, but thereafter the engine was never so well tuned and right at the end of the year he scraped together enough cash to buy a current Brabham, and showed well in his only race with it before spinning off the road.

In the following season the tall Swede with the spectacular, karting style learned all about Formula 3 racing in the Brabham, and then bought one of the new short-wheelbase Tecno cars from the Italian kart company.

He knew the Pederzani brothers, who ran Tecno, from his karting days, and in the two seasons of 1968 and 1969 he shone in his privately-owned car. During the earlier season he raced mainly in Sweden while his friendly rival Reine Wisell drove a Tecno very successfully in the European circus.

In 1969 Ronnie took his new, yellow-painted Tecno onto the European circuits, racing a lot in Italy, while Wisell drove mainly in England for the works Chevron team. Peterson had become the man to beat in Formula 3, with Wisell and Australian Tim Schenken — who was to become a flat-mate and close friend of Ronnie's — close behind him.

In England, the March Engineering car company was slowly being constituted, and its founders had decided that they would like either Peterson or Wisell to drive for them, and decided to choose whichever won the major Monaco Formula 3 race. It was the first Peterson-Wisell meeting of the season, and each won his respective heat to start side-by-side on the front row of the grid for the Final. The two Swedes battled furiously around the houses, passing and repassing until Wisell missed the chicane and skated down an escape road, leaving Peterson to steam home and win.

Shortly afterwards, at London's Crystal Palace circuit, Peterson was second to Schenken, and there he met Alan Rees, an ex-racing driver who was at that time managing the Winkelmann Brabham Formula 2 team. Rees was one of the founder directors of the March concern, and he asked Peterson to see him in his office at Slough the next day.

Ronnie found his way there, and Rees asked him to drive one of Winkelmann's F2 Brabhams at Albi and mentioned that he had a deal coming up which could include Formula 2 and Formula 1 rides. Ronnie did not speak much English, but he knew what 'Formula One' meant, and he pricked up his ears.

He had already had a rather disastrous Formula 2 debut in a works Tecno, wiping it out against the Armco at Monza, but he drove well at Albi and then gave the very first prototype Formula 3 March its debut at the end of that season. He was third at Cadwell Park, but then crashed heavily at Montlhéry when dazzled by the late-afternoon sun.

He was lying in hospital, recovering from bruising and slight burns and thinking 'I've missed my schance' when the March directors appeared with a contract for 1970. He signed.

Ronnie was to have been the new manufacturer's first Formula 1 driver, and when Chris Amon was signed on he should have become number two. But meanwhile Jo Siffert came along with Porsche money backing him, and he took the second seat in the works team.

March could easily have ditched their promising nobody, but instead they arranged a private Formula 1 ride for him in a car entered by Colin Crabbe's Antique Automobiles company. It was a low-budget operation, but it gave Peterson a perfect, low-key, low-pressure entry into the world of Formula 1, which earned him seventh place at Monaco, first time out.

During that season he found his feet in Formula 1, and proved as quick as anybody in Formula 2 despite driving a rather inferior spaceframe March. The car was good on any fast circuit where it did not need much wing, and at Rouen he led all the established Formula 2 aces — including Jochen Rindt — until he spun off halfway round the last lap.

In many ways Ronnie was very like Rindt; the same wild-looking style, lurid cornering repeated with complete consistency on every lap; the same indomitable spirit when problems struck his machinery; and the same off-hand — if rather more politely uninformative — attitude to the popular Press. While Rindt's early years in Formula 1 had been with uncompetitive Coopers, Ronnie's were with less-than-competitive Marches, and he stayed with the Bicester team into 1971. During this second season with the team he proved his potential, continually running second behind Stewart to become runner-up to him in the World Championship; in 1972, once March had scrapped their experimental 721X car and had turned to a Formula 2-based model, Ronnie came back to take one third and a fourth place in a disappointing season.

Typical Peterson – forcing his obsolete Lotus 72 beyond its natural limits he rushes round Monaco on his way to victory in the 1974 GP. His successes that season at Monaco, Dijon and Monza displayed his talents on vastly different types of circuit

Meanwhile he had been racing and winning in Formula 2, and had been earning quite big money as one of the Ferrari sports car team drivers. Late in 1971 he had driven for Alfa Romeo in the Watkins Glen 6-Hours, and had won the race. The new Ferrari 312P prototype was running in the same event, and in typical style Peterson considered that although the Alfa must be the car to win during the following season, the Ferrari – which had been breaking with monotonous regularity – looked like being more fun to drive. So he signed with Ferrari, they gained reliability while Alfa Romeo lost it, and Ronnie found himself winning a string of endurance classics – much to his surprise – with Tim Schenken.

During this period he had his problems. He had twice crashed heavily in Formula 1 Marches, once in testing at Ontario and once in the non-Championship race at Silverstone where the throttle stuck and powered him head-on into a retaining bank. In that accident he was badly concussed, and there were many others during the season, including some in Formula 2.

He had a reputation for being extremely fast, but some suggested that he was totally brainless – his slow manner out of the car, his mild smile, even-temper and slow, measured speech convinced them that this was so. Some said if you looked hard into his blue eyes you could see straight out the back of his head.

But his sheer speed in a car made

him a hot property, and at the end of 1972 he accepted a lucrative offer from Colin Chapman and the John Player Lotus team to join them for the following season. Max Mosley of March made no secret of his feelings; 'He's had 14 accidents with us this year, and frankly we can't afford him. I only hope that Chapman has plenty of cars for him to use up . . .' That was an outburst of sour grapes.

Early in the new season Peterson did look expensive, for although his Lotus 72 continually failed under his driving, he always had little in reserve, gave of his best *all* the time, and whenever the unexpected happened his cat-like reflexes were not always sufficient to save his car.

Whereas a Fangio or a Moss might have foreseen a situation, Peterson did not, and he crashed heavily at Silverstone when put off line by a smaller car on test, and then had a terrible time at the Belgian Grand Prix when he put his two cars on pole position and shunted them both in the pre-race setting-up session, and then crashed his race car after leading the early laps. He had a fever that day, and should not really have driven, but his learning graph was rising.

As the team made his cars strong enough to withstand the enormous loadings he induced, Peterson became a winner. He was leading fair and square in Austria before waving Fittipaldi through to save his chance of retaining the Championship, and

Ronnie was genuinely sorry when the Brazilian's car broke and gave Peterson his second Grand Prix victory instead.

At Monza a win for Fittipaldi represented his last chance of staying in the Championship, but when Ronnie saw a pit signal that Stewart was up into fourth place he understood that Emerson's last chance had gone anyway, and he tore on to that controversial victory, 0·8-second ahead of his joint number one.

Fittipaldi had bowed to enormous pressure from his effusive Brazilian followers and advisors, and his normally equable facade began to crumble as he was heard to complain darkly that Peterson was receiving preferential treatment. By this time the Swede's self-confidence was total, and he knew that he could not only drive a Formula 1 car faster than any other man (including Fittipaldi and Stewart), but he could also win Grands Prix in it.

This was an important plus, and team manager Peter Warr was astonished by the Swede's mild temperament in practice in Canada, where he qualified on his eighth pole position of the year. Goodyear had only one set of special intermediate tyres available for what was to be a rain-marred race, and Warr argued long and hard for a second set to fulfil his obligations to his two joint number one drivers.

The tyre company felt that the sole set of tyres should go to Peterson, on pole, for Fittipaldi was well down the grid. The Brazilian was understandably agitated, and Ronnie sensed trouble and asked what was going on. When Warr told him of the tyre problem, his reaction was immediate, and natural; 'Let Emerson have them', he said, 'I'll win whatever you give me . . . !'

He did not win, but such nobility fully demonstrated his newfound stature as the fastest man of his time. He had been a cross between the racing fire and fury of a Jochen Rindt, and the quietly amiable introversion of a Jimmy Clark. Now he had begun to temper his sheer speed and an unquenchable will to win with broad experience, and just beneath that rather shy, mild and very likable exterior there lurked an increasingly thoughtful racing driver, and an astute professional sense.

In 1974 the new Lotus 76 proved a failure, and Ronnie hurled all his skill into keeping the ageing Lotus 72s competitive. He won at Monaco, at Dijon and at Monza, on three of the most divergent circuits one could imagine, and he went into 1975 convinced that all he needed to become the first Swedish World Champion driver was some of that elusive luck. . .

It rapidly became obvious that Ronnie would virtually have to rely on luck alone, for the Lotus 72 was by this time far too heavy and far too old. It had been conceived for 1970 tyres and conditions, had been modified successfully up to 1973, Ronnie virtually carried it on his shoulders through 1974 and now the opposition were just too far ahead with cars purpose-built to make the most of Goodyear's latest tyres. He managed to score Championship points with fourth place at Monaco, and two fifths in Austria and at Watkins Glen, and still showed occasional flashes of brilliance although some of his undemonstrative Scandinavian competitiveness seemed to have drained away.

The new Lotus 77 for 1976 was beset with initial development problems, and after the Brazilian race Ronnie succeeded in terminating his contract and returning to March. Throughout the 1975 season March fans had been predicting great things should Ronnie return to handle the F2-derived cars, but his first few races for the Bicester outfit were muted. From mid-season the old Peterson emerged, and he led race after race at some point before finally enjoying the mechanical reliability to finish at Monza — first for the third time in the Italian GP.

Ronnie Peterson signed to drive for the ELF Tyrrell team of six-wheel cars in 1977, and looked all set to emulate Jackie Stewart's huge success in their colours. He could still be the best racing driver around in the mid-1970s, but he has to prove it.

Four of the Best

Winning the World Championship calls for a combination of skill and good fortune. Four drivers who won the title more than once could not be ranked in the same supreme bracket with Fangio or Clark, but between them they shared 53 *Grande Epreuve* victories plus many more of the sport's top honours. As multiple World Champions, Alberto Ascari, Jack Brabham, Graham Hill and Emerson Fittipaldi are surely four of the very best . . .

Alberto Ascari
BORN JULY 13, 1918, MILAN, ITALY

During the two seasons of 1952 and 1953, when Formula 1 was dead on its feet and the World Championship was run for 2-litre unsupercharged Formula 2 cars, Alberto Ascari reigned supreme. He drove his dominant four-cylinder Ferraris to 11 Grand Prix victories in 14 starts, and took the World title by a large margin in both seasons.

It was the fulfilment of a promise born into the burly, genial and very popular Italian, for his father had been the great Antonio Ascari, killed in his Alfa Romeo while leading the French Grand Prix on July 26, 1925.

Alberto was barely seven at the time of his father's death, but he immediately grasped the enormity of his loss; no more rides in the works Alfa Romeos at Monza, no more of that expansive affection with which Latin fathers cherish their sons; no more small boy stories of his father's latest race wins and daring escapades . . . no more 'Papa'. . .

Eliza Ascari brought up Alberto and his sister on her own, and began fearing for her son's future when he was 11 and already scorching around nearby streets on a friend's motor cycle. He hated the schools to which he was sent, and worked out all kinds of schemes to save enough money to

An ebullient 'Ciccio' Ascari celebrates high on his mechanics' shoulders after winning the 1951 Italian GP at Monza

hire a motor cycle on which to practice in the holidays. He was moved from school to school in an effort to distract his interest from the type of sport which had claimed his father, but when he was 18 his mother finally bowed to the inevitable.

Ascari had absconded from school, and had telephoned his mother to say that he saw his future in racing motor cycles, it was the only thing he wanted to do. She climbed down and helped him to buy a 500 cc Sertum.

He made his debut with this machine on June 28, 1936, in a 24-Hour Reliability Trial across northern Italy. He fell off. One week later he attempted a Regularity Test at Lario, and won his class.

During the next three years, Ascari became a works Bianchi rider and was increasingly anxious to progress to racing cars as had his father and the great ex-motor-cyclists Nuvolari and Varzi. He had set-up a petroleum transport business which helped his exemption from National Service at 21, and in April 1940 Enzo Ferrari asked him to drive one of a pair of '815' 1½-litre sports cars in the Mille Miglia circuit race of that year. The '815', built by a cover company named Auto Avio Costruzzioni, was in fact the first Ferrari – the *Commendatore* being prohibited from giving his own name to a car under the terms of his recent severance contract with Alfa Romeo.

Ascari shared the drive with his cousin, Franco Minozzi, who was an experienced Alfa Romeo driver, and they were leading their class easily after more than 90 miles when the valve gear of the 815's engine failed.

An exciting trip to North Africa followed, in which Ascari Junior finished ninth in a Maserati 6C in the Tripoli Voiturette race, and he then retired in the Targa Florio – run that year for Voiturettes in Palermo's Favorita Park.

Then Italy entered the war, and Ascari's company earned him a reserved occupation which kept him out of the forces. When peace returned to Europe, Alberto Ascari was a married man of 27, with a small son named Antonio, and a bursting ambition to get back into motor racing.

He returned in 1947, driving in Piero Dusio's Cisitalia D46 'circus' on Gezirah Island at Cairo in Egypt. He was second to Taruffi in his heat and to Cortese in the Final, and this performance earned him an invitation to join the Scuderia Ambrosiana works Maserati team later that year.

There 'Ciccio' as he was known became a close friend and pupil of Luigi Villoresi, who began to instil much of his own smooth, effortless style into this very fast but rather untidy new-

'Ascari–Ferrari' sounds right and, winning or not, looked right. Here at Barcelona in 1951 he did not win, placing fourth behind two Alfa Romeos (which clinched the World title for Fangio) and his team-mate Gonzalez who briefly overshadowed him

Speed with style – Ascari Jr opposite-locks his all-conquering Ferrari 500 on its way to winning the 1952 British GP at Silverstone

comer. Everywhere he raced, the new Ascari showed promise, but his Maseratis were unreliable. Then in September at Modena he was leading Villoresi in the new cycle-winged A6G Maseratis when the race was stopped after a competing car had charged a spectator area. It was Alberto Ascari's first victory on four wheels.

At San Remo, early in 1948, Ascari beat his mentor fair-and-square to give the 4CLT/48 Maserati its debut with a 1–2 finish, and to give the car its nickname as the 'San Remo Maserati'. Thereafter Villoresi did the winning, while Ascari led the Mille Miglia and won the Coppa Acerbo in A6Gs.

Partly in tribute to his father's memory and partly in respect for his increasing skill, Alfa Romeo gave him a drive in the French Grand Prix at Reims, and he came home third – to team orders.

By the 1949 season it was clear that Ascari was embarrassingly faster than Villoresi, who had coached him unstintingly, but the two remained firm friends and after a successful South American tour with Maserati they returned to Europe and joined the Ferrari camp, where Alberto attained his full maturity as a racing driver.

During that 1949 season his burly, big-breasted figure in dark blue shirt and light-blue linen helmet was a familiar sight leading Grand Prix races

in the 1½-litre supercharged Ferraris; he won the Swiss and Italian Grands Prix and the International Trophy race at Silverstone.

His style was now fully developed, smooth, undemonstrative, but extremely fast and lap after lap he would nip the same kerb stone with perfect consistency, brown arms flicking the steering as he made his car do what he wanted and prevented it doing what it wanted.

During 1950 Alfa Romeo reappeared on the scene, to dominate Grand Prix racing, but Ascari's Ferraris cleaned-up in Formula 2 events and his big unsupercharged 4½-litre car won the Spanish Grand Prix. With this machine he took the German and Italian Grands Prix during Alfa's last season of 1951, and with the new Formula 2 World Championship races in 1952 and 1953 Ascari had a ready-made race winner in the Ferrari 500.

His car was superior to most of his competitors', but this friendly, warm man drove with exceptional skill and used his head to achieve a well-earned domination which was total. He had missed the first 2-litre Grand Prix, at Berne, as he was at Indianapolis where he was forced to retire in the '500' after his Ferrari 375 broke a wheel.

For 1954 Gianni Lancia attracted Ascari and Villoresi away from Ferrari to drive his new 2½-litre V8 cars, but they were a long time coming, and the double World Champion's talents lay largely fallow apart from the Mille Miglia which he won in a Lancia D24. His services were loaned to Maserati for the French and British Grands Prix and to Ferrari for the Italian, but at Reims and Silverstone he retired, and at Monza suffered engine failure after leading.

The strikingly small new Lancia made its debut in the last race of the season, at Barcelona, and Ascari immediately qualified it on pole position, but was out after ten laps with clutch trouble.

Into 1955 the Lancia was competitive with the Mercedes, and Ascari led the Argentine Grand Prix before spinning off, for his new mount was unforgiving as well as fast. Ascari then won the non-Championship races at Turin and Naples, and led at Pau before the next Grand Prix at Monaco.

There he was about to take the lead as Moss retired the last surviving Mercedes at its pit. It was the 80th lap and Ascari's wine-red Lancia came bulleting out of the *Tir aux Pigeons* tunnel, flicked down into the chicane on the quayside and then broadsided as the right front brake locked, crashed wildly through a straw bale barrier,

bounced off a bollard and plunged into Monte Carlo Harbour.

Horrified spectators heaved a sigh of relief as Ascari's blue helmet bobbed to the surface, and the Italian ace struck out strongly to be picked up by a rescue boat. His nose and back were battered and bruised, he was soaked and shocked but otherwise unhurt. Down on the harbour bed his battered Lancia could be seen clearly through the crystal water.

Four days later, on May 26, he was at Monza, looking for a drive to test his reactions to the accident. Unofficial testing was under way for the Supercortemaggiore sports car race, and 'Ciccio' was gladly loaned a 3-litre Ferrari by his old team.

On his third lap he went missing. The Ferrari had spun wildly on entering the Vialone Curve at well over 100 mph, had been tripped by the grass verge and had rolled over and over. Ascari died in the ambulance, with Villoresi — in deep shock — by his side.

Like his father before him, the first double World Champion had been killed in a largely inexplicable accident, on the 26 of the month, at the age of 36, and had left behind him a wife and two small children. He was a good man, deeply mourned.

John Arthur 'Jack' Brabham
BORN APRIL 2, 1926, HURSTVILLE, NEW SOUTH WALES, AUSTRALIA

If his contemporaries like Moss, Clark and Stewart were motor racing thoroughbreds, then Jack Brabham was a supremely successful blacksmith. He was an intensely practical, wily driver-cum-engineer, and in his 16 seasons of International racing he drove in 126 Grands Prix, won 14 of of them, was three-times World Champion Driver, and twice took credit as World Champion Constructor. He was the first of the modern drivers to build his own racing cars, the first to win a *Grande Epreuve* in a car bearing his own name, and the first to take the Championship in his own car.

In the process, this tough, silent, secretive man also made himself a considerable fortune in a guarded and

'Black Jack' — motor racing's wiliest World Champion

unpublicised manner which left few people in any doubt; *nobody* in modern motor racing has been a brighter operator than 'Black Jack' Brabham.

He was a second generation Australian, whose grandfather had been a Cockney from Bow in East London. His father ran a grocery store outside Sydney, and Jack was an only child, with a typically outdoor Australian upbringing. Father was a keen motorist, and he taught Jack to drive when he was about 12, using the family Chevrolet and the grocery business' trucks. He left school at 15, and went to work in a garage, while studying engineering in the evenings at Kogarah Tech.

In 1944, when he was 18, Brabham joined the Royal Australian Air Force, and he served for two years as ground crew before starting a tiny motor repair business in 1946. It was at this time that he met an American living in Sydney named Johnny Schonberg. He raced midget cars, and for 1947 Brabham helped build him a new classis and engineered a new engine for it in his growing little business.

When Schonberg's wife persuaded him to stop racing, Brabham took over the midget, was taught how to drive it on Tempe mud flats and then made his race debut at Paramatta

Brabham's Cooper at Spa where he won the 1960 Belgian Grand Prix — the second of his run of five consecutive victories in that his second World Championsip season

Park Speedway. After three nights racing he was acclimatised to the rough and tumble, gritty, dusty world of midget racing, and he won the feature race.

In his first season he won the New South Wales Championship at Sydney Showground, and he lost the South Australian title one bleak night in Adelaide when the midget's special engine literally exploded and caught fire.

It was the end of his midget racing, but in the meantime he had tried his hand in a few hill-climbs and had met an enthusiastic young engineer named Ron Tauranac who was building hill-climb specials at home with his brother Austin. These dry, taciturn characters were kindred spirits to Brabham, and in 1951 they prompted him to take up hill-climbing seriously.

He resurrected the old Midget, and encountered bitter opposition from the conservative road racing purists as he stormed to victory in the Australian Hill-Climb Championship. Their reception for a 'tearaway' from the dirt tracks can be imagined, and there was a certain amount of needle in Jack's subsequent decision to buy a Cooper-JAP 1100 and take them on at their own game. He was successful enough to gain backing from RedeX, the addi-

tive people, and they helped finance a Cooper-Bristol. The Australian sporting authority objected strongly to RedeX advertising on the car, and so Brabham took it to New Zealand with the Queensland and NSW Road Racing titles to his name.

He was sixth with the car in the 1954 New Zealand Grand Prix, and returned the following season when he met Dick Jeffrey of Dunlop and Dean Delamont of the British RAC who persuaded him to try his skills in Europe.

So he came to England, leaving his wife and young son at home in case things did not work out. He put his faith in a Cooper-Alta which was diabolically unreliable, but his spectacular dirt track style endeared him to the crowds at circuits like Goodwood and Ibsley. He met the Coopers, father and son, and with their blessing built himself a rear-engined 2-litre Cooper-Bristol with which he made his World

Championship debut in the British Grand Prix at Aintree.

Jack invested in a Maserati 250F, for the 1956 Formula 1 season, which proved to be a mistake, and later joined the Cooper works team as a Formula 2 driver, and took part in several Championship rounds, in the F2 class when there was one, or with 2·2-litre engines as a hybrid F1 car.

By 1959 the little Coopers were running full 2½-litre engines, and the dark-shaven Australian with his forceful, crouching style won at Monaco and in Britain, amassing enough points elsewhere to win the Championship in dramatic style by pushing his out-of-fuel car across the line in the United States Grand Prix at Sebring.

The 1960 season was even more of a Brabham triumph, for whereas he had clinched the 1959 title by the skin of his teeth, in this new season he won five consecutive *Grandes*

Superb study of Jack Brabham in full cry at the Nürburgring

Epreuves to leave nobody in any doubt about the combination of Brabham and his mid-engined Cooper-Climax.

When 1½-litre Formula 1 racing began in 1961, the British teams were handicapped by the slow introduction of competitive engines, and it was Brabham who drove the first Climax V8, at the Nürburgring, and smartly reversed the lot through a hedge on the opening lap.

By the end of the season it was obvious that Cooper, who had pioneered the rear-engined revolution in Grand Prix racing, had been left behind, and Brabham had backed a new production racing car venture named Motor Racing Developments. building Formula Junior cars designed by Ron Tauranac.

At this time the Brabham garage empire was growing in both Australia and England, and in mid-1962 the first Brabham Formula 1 car made its debut, and fifth place in the United States Grand Prix yielded the first Championship points ever won by a driver in a car of his own manufacture.

For the remaining three seasons of the 1½-litre Formula the Brabham Racing Organisation team was formed, with Jack being joined by the lanky American ace, Dan Gurney. Their first Formula 1 victories came quickly, in the 1963 non-Championship events at Solitude in Germany and Zeltweg in Austria, but Grand Prix success proved elusive until the French Grand Prix of 1964, which Gurney won with Brabham a delighted third.

As pressure of business increased, Brabham went into partial retirement during 1965, hoping for new driver Denny Hulme to take his place, but it was a largely luckless season and when Gurney went off to build his own Eagle cars for the new 3-litre Formula in 1966, Jack was back in full harness.

He drove his modestly powerful, intensely practical, Repco-Brabham to win the French, British, Dutch and German Grands Prix, and became the first driver other than Fangio to become triple World Champion. In this supreme season his Brabham-Honda Formula 2 car tore the class apart, winning nine times to take the *Grands Prix de France* Championship. That year Brabham's teams won literally hundreds of bottles of Champagne. Evidently it was typical of Jack that nobody else saw the going of them.

In 1967 Denny Hulme took the World title in revised Repco-Brabhams, with Jack runner-up and winner of the French and Canadian races. Then in 1968 Jochen Rindt joined the team, they had a sorry time with new four-cam Repco V8s, and suffered a wretched season.

That year saw Brabham running at Indianapolis for the first time since 1964, when he had the narrowest escape of his racing life. He had driven one of his own cars, powered by an Offenhauser engine, through the second lap fireball which stopped the race and killed two drivers. It was hardly surprising he took four years to return. Back in 1961 he had raced there with a 2·7-litre Cooper-Climax, placed ninth, and had astonished the Indy establishment with this funny little rear-engined green-painted car . . . To the superstitious Indy establishment its green paint was even more heretic than the engine mounting. . . .

If the purse was big enough, Brabham would always put his heart into a race, and in 1969 he turned to the Cosworth-Ford engine and drove hard and well in support of his young Belgian team-mate Jacky Ickx. But Jack broke his left ankle in a bad mid-season testing accident at Silverstone, where he had won a rain-soaked International Trophy earlier in the year. Now he was out of the game until the Italian Grand Prix.

He had long been thinking of retirement, but the non-availability of top-line drivers had kept him driving. Now 1970 was to be his last season — his 23rd year in the game — and it started brilliantly with victory in South Africa, first time out in a new monocoque car.

The 1966 season was a Brabham triumph as apart from the third World Championship title team-mates Jack and Denny Hulme dominated Formula 2 racing with their Brabham-Hondas. Here at Reims, during the first GP win weekend, Denny gives the Guv'nor a Formula 2 tow

He should have won at least twice more, at Monaco and Brands Hatch, but a stunning lapse at the Mediterranean resort put him into the straw bales on the last corner while leading, and in the British Grand Prix he found the measure of Rindt's Lotus, stormed by and was pacing himself to victory when his car ran out of fuel halfway round the last lap! He was second in both races, and after late season troubles was fifth in his last World Championship. His last race before retirement was the Mexican Grand Prix, and there he was running third when his engine failed.

Jack Brabham's racing career was extraordinary. Throughout it he remained fiercely competitive, and he always knew when to race and when merely to drive fast enough to conserve a car or a place. If a car failed him he could either butcher it mercilessly or, if the stakes were high, nurse it to the finish like a baby. His dirt track style moderated as he matured, but when the chips were down he would hurl his cars around, showering pursuers with dust and stones in a most un-compromising manner. There was a story that his bulging top overall pocket contained his favourite boiled sweets. Numerous rivals who retired with holed radiators mumbled darkly of flying pebbles ... Nobody was as hard as Black Jack on a black day.

Racing sports cars was an infrequent relaxation — after early drives for Aston Martin and in his Cooper Monacos, in his final season he enjoyed being one of Matra's 'hired men' without the responsibility of team ownership on his shoulders.

He was also a great private flyer, with a succession of aircraft, and every move he made had a carefully considered motive behind it. In his last two seasons he was a much more open, more extrovert personality, but he really did not need to be. Thousands turned out for the Brands Hatch farewell meeting held in his honour, and that was a tribute to motor racing's great elder statesman, the veteran who never passed his peak and who knew when the joke was over. He was far more popular than perhaps he ever knew. . .

Norman Graham Hill

BORN FEBRUARY 15, 1929, HAMPSTEAD, LONDON, ENGLAND

Graham Hill — British World Champion in 1962 and 1968

The best ambassador the sport ever had, is a much-used and rather hackneyed phrase, but it suited Graham Hill perfectly. From his Grand Prix debut at Reims in 1958 to his retirement in 1975 he had driven in a record-shattering 176 Championship-qualifying races, had won 14 of them, had twice become World Champion Driver, and was the only man ever to have won the World title, the Indianapolis 500 and also the Le Mans 24-Hours classic.

He was at his peak in the years of $1\frac{1}{2}$-litre Formula 1 (1961–65), he won his second Championship in a hard-fought title chase in 1968 and after his come-back following a bad accident late in 1969 was a shadow of his former self. He continued because he was still enjoying it, and still receiving due popular acclaim wherever he raced, but to those who remembered him at his height every also-ran performance was agonising to behold.

Graham Hill started driving late, and was never a born natural racing driver, like Moss or Clark or Stewart. He achieved his standing by sheer dedication and determined hard work.

As a boy he was educated at Hendon Technical College, and took a five-year apprenticeship with Smiths Instruments, who despatched him to a study centre in Cheltenham. He had a 1936 Velocette motor cycle, and one dark night rode it into a stationary car up in the Cotswolds while on his way home to London.

The result was a fractured thigh, poorly treated, which left him with a left leg half-an-inch shorter than the other and a limp to match. He had ridden in a few scrambles and trials on the Velocette, but now he took to rowing as a sport before National Service saw him conscripted into the Navy in 1950. He served two years, mostly as an engine room artificer in HMS *Swiftsure*, and then returned to Smiths and to the London Rowing Club whose colours he later carried on his crash helmet.

He was nearly 24 when he bought his first car, a distinctly evil 1934 Morris 8 Tourer, and after just two weeks of self-instructed driving Graham Hill passed his test and became legitimate. Late that year he saw an advertisement for the Universal Motor Racing Club at Brands Hatch, and he joined, paid a pound and had four exciting and significant laps in a worn-out Cooper-JAP '500'. Club organiser Gordon Thornton took him on as part-time helper, and when Thornton vanished and the Club collapsed Graham had left Smiths and talked himself into another honorary job preparing two cars belonging to another would-be racing drivers' school proprietor.

At this time the future World Champion was surviving on National Assistance and help from his mother, and taking a bus down to Westerham every day to work on the cars. On April 27, 1954 his employer paid him his fee, a drive in a Mark 4 Cooper-JAP in a race at Brands Hatch.

Soon after this debut he met Colin Chapman and went to work for his embryo Lotus company in a stable in Hornsey, North London, and then became mechanic to Dick Steed and later to Dan Margulies, who raced Lotus and Jaguar cars around Europe.

When he married he went to work full-time for Lotus, and in his spare time worked as a racing mechanic for anybody who would give him a drive in return. Early in 1956 he built up his own Lotus 11 with encouragement from Colin Chapman, and he led the *Autosport* club racing Championship with it until its engine failed in the final race. In the following season he raced all manner of cars for various owners, and in 1957 he drove briefly for the Cooper works team before returning to Chapman as a works Lotus driver.

In 1958 the Lotus 12s appeared in Grand Prix racing, and in his debut, at Monaco, Graham was running fourth until a rear wheel fell off. That set the style for his Lotus Formula 1 outings, and by the end of 1959 he had had enough of their cars' fragility and moved to BRM.

With them he found the ill-handling rear-engined cars being blown-off by his previous season's number two driver, Innes Ireland, in the latest rear-engined Lotus 18s. It was a galling experience, but at Silverstone Hill led the British GP until six laps from the end, when he spun off and stalled.

Meanwhile he was continuing to drive in Formula 2 and in any sports or saloon cars which came along, notably for Porsche, and at the end of the 1961 season — in which the BRMs struggled with $1\frac{1}{2}$-litre Coventry Climax four-cylinder engines — Graham Hill was 13th in the World Championship and seemed to be just another run-of-the-mill GP driver hamstrung by his machinery.

But the 1962 season saw his mask-like determination and bristling moustache in the latest BRM V8s, winning the pre-season meetings at Goodwood and Silverstone (where he virtually dead-heated with Jimmy Clark) and then going on to victory in the Dutch, German, Italian and South African Grands Prix to pip Clark narrowly for the Championship.

Right: Hill's greatest drive – his BRM leads Surtees' Lola and Gurney's Porsche round the North Curve at the Nürburgring during the wet 1962 German GP. His win helped him and his team to their joint first World Championship titles

Below: Lady Luck smiled on Graham Hill when he won the 1966 Indianapolis 500 in one of John Mecom's Lola–Ford T90s, but he remains the only driver ever to have won Indy, the World Drivers' Championship and the Le Mans 24-Hours in a unique motor racing 'Triple Crown'

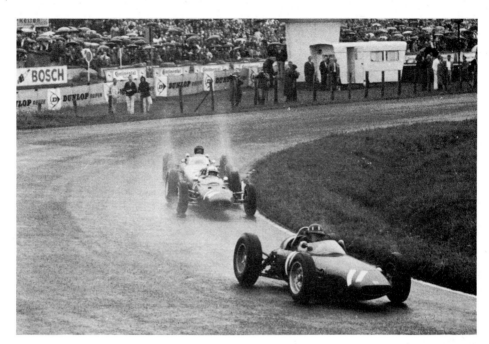

He seemed a fixture at BRM by this time, and was to stay with them for four more seasons, scoring three consecutive wins in both the Monaco and United States Grands Prix, nurturing the young Jackie Stewart and working, working all the time to perfect his car and to sharpen his driving. His intense, almost trance-like application made his cars do what he wanted. While starring in Formula 1 with his continuing battle with Jimmy Clark he amassed a vast string of successes in sports and GT and saloon car events of anything from 10-laps to 12-hours duration.

He was runner-up in the World Championship in 1963–4–5, and actually scored more points than John Surtees in the 1964 season only to lose two on the best performances 'tax' system; a loss which made Surtees the Champion by one point. . .

In 1963 he had practised a Mickey Thompson car at Indianapolis, and three years later he scored a fairly lucky win there in one of John Mecom's Lola-Fords, buying himself a twin-engined aircraft from the proceeds. From that point forwards 'Hillarious Airways' was in business 'seriously'. . .

That 1966 season had seen BRM beset by troubles with their H16 engine, and for the following year Graham returned to Lotus, attracted by Ford money to become Jimmy Clark's joint number one.

They proved a formidable pair in their new Lotus-Ford 49s, but Graham in particular had a heart-breaking series of tantalising failures which kept him out of the winner's circle. After Jimmy's death, which Hill could scarcely credit, he brought Lotus bounding back with consecutive wins in Spain and at Monaco, and clinched the Championship in the last race in Mexico. It was his second title, and his superb public image as the waggish, articulate Londoner, gave full value.

In 1969 he won at Monaco for a staggering fifth time in seven years, underlining his enormous powers of sheer concentration, his stamina and his great mechanical sympathy, but he was less competitive for the rest of the season, being overshadowed by Jochen Rindt, his new team-mate. At Watkins Glen he spun and restarted without being able to re-fasten his seat belts. A tyre was deflating, and he lost control again as he was about to come into the pits. This time the Gold Leaf Lotus somersaulted and threw him out, breaking his right knee, dislocating the left and damaging some vital ligaments.

Master of Monaco — no other driver as yet approaches Graham's record of five Monte Carlo victories. He scored his last Monaco win in this Lotus 49B in 1969

He was in hospital for some months, and the wave of public sympathy in Britain was enormous for he was by far the most popular racing driver we had. Against doctor's orders he was racing again in the South African Grand Prix in March, 1970, when he could barely walk, yet he was placed sixth in Rob Walker's private Lotus.

From that time forward he seldom achieved anything like his old stature, driving for Brabham in 1971–72 – and winning the International Trophy Silverstone for them – and in his own Shadow and Lola cars with Embassy cigarette brand backing from 1973–75. In the 1973 season with the white and red Shadow he scored no World Championship points (by failing to finish in the first six in any Championship GP) but he more than compensated by winning the 1972 Le Mans 24-Hours race in a Matra-Simca.

He looked all set to go through the 200 Grand Prix barrier, and insisted he would go on racing as long as he found he was still enjoying it. His Embassy-backed team designed and built their own Hill-Cosworth cars for the major part of the 1975 season, and Rolf Stommelen was leading the Spanish GP at Barcelona in the proto-type before its rear wing collapsed and hurled the German into an horrific accident which killed several on-lookers. In that same race a newcomer named Tony Brise proved himself a budding F1 ace, and Graham signed him on to join the Australian Alan Jones in his team. 'With youngsters quicker than myself around it wasn't fair to hog the cockpit' he said, and announced his retirement from driving.

To many of his supporters this came as a relief, but on the night of November 29, 1975, the Hill Racing executive aircraft ploughed into the grasping branches of an ancient elm tree on Arkley Golf Course, North London, on its approach to Elstree Aerodrome where Graham based it. He was returning from shake-down testing of his new 1976 Hill GH2 at the Ricard-Castellet circuit in the South of France. Graham Hill, double World Champion Driver, Indy 500 and Le Mans winner, perished in the crash, and Tony Brise, team manager, team designer and two mechanics died with him. Such a fate was not altogether un-expected for the most popular of all postwar British racing drivers, but it was bitterly tragic that his whole team should be snuffed out with him.

Emerson Fittipaldi
BORN DECEMBER 12, 1946, SÃO PAULO, BRAZIL

A driver with brains; Emerson Fittipaldi – Brazil's double World Champion, with Lotus in 1972, with McLaren in 1974

Son of a motor racing journalist, the personable, astute Brazilian became the youngest World Champion yet when he took the title with sheer brilliance in 1972. He had driven his John Player-backed Lotus 72 to five Grand Prix wins and added four more first places in non-Championship rounds before the year was out. His return to Brazil was greeted by de-lirious crowds of well-wishers, and at 26 he had become as giant a national figure as Pele. In the following season misfortune lost him his title while Stewart's seasoned skills took it, and then in 1974 he tigered when he had to, trod softly when he had to, and stole his second Championship in the last of the fifteen qualifying rounds. Brazil's cup of pride overflowed . . .

Fittipaldi Sr had tried his hand at competition, but the attempt ended in 1952 when he had a bad accident on a 500 cc BMW motor cycle. Thereafter Papa seems to have been torn between his ambitions for his two sons to do well in the sport which fascinated him so much, and a paternal fear for their safety.

So when Emerson wanted to go motor-cycle racing he was limited to 50 cc machines, and simultaneously he was mechanic for elder brother Wilson's karts. He was only 15 when he had his first taste of competition riding, and at 17 he was out in his own kart and a year later fought his way to become the local Champion of 1965.

Wilson, three years older, had started driving Alpine GTs for the local Renault assembly plant, and the same team took on young Emerson to race their Dauphines, in which he won the novice championship.

Meanwhile Wilson had returned dispirited from a brief foray into European racing, and with him he brought a leather-clad steering wheel. There was no such device in Brazil at the time, and the brothers set-up their own goody shop, making and selling all kinds of 'go-faster' items.

In 1966 the brothers built their own 'Minikarts' and ran a team which won everything in sight. At the end of the year Emerson took in a series of long-distance races in a locally-built special, and then in 1967 his karting took second place to the newly-introduced Formula Vee. The brothers built the Fitti-Vee which Emerson promptly drove to five wins in the seven-race Championship series to take the Brazilian title, then added the karting Championship in a 125 cc Minikart, and second in the GT Championship in a Porsche-engined Karmann Ghia Volkswagen.

A home-built Porsche GT followed, and in May 1969 Emerson Fittipaldi arrived in England with just enough capital to buy a Formula Ford Merlyn and one of Deny Rowland's good engines. His first race was at Zandvoort, and he was leading his heat when the engine failed. A win at Snetterton followed, and with three wins out of nine events he was offered a Lotus Formula 3 ride by racing school proprietor, Jim Russell.

Typical Fittipaldi progress showed in his Formula 3 career. In his first race he was fifth, in his second he was third and he won the next time out. His first European victory was at Montlhéry and he ended the half-season as Lombank F3 Champion.

At this stage he spoke very little English, he just drove, and he drove with an even calm and unspectacular

Before the head took over from the heart — Fittipaldi gaining experience of turbine power and four-wheel drive in a non-Championship Formula 1 race; Brands Hatch, 1971

skill and cunning which marked him as a true ace in the making.

In 1970 he was into Formula 2 with a Lotus-Cosworth, and that May saw Colin Chapman giving him a Formula 1 test drive. By the time of the British Grand Prix he was signed on as a third team member, with Rindt and John Miles, and he made his debut at Brands Hatch in the Gold Leaf team's old-nail Lotus 49. He was eighth. Next time out, in Germany, he was fourth to score his first points; in Austria he had trouble; in Italy he crashed mildly in practice, before Rindt's death caused the team to withdraw; in his next race — his fourth Grand Prix — in America he *won*. It was the season's richest race, it was Team Lotus' comeback after the Monza tragedy, and it clinched their posthumous Championship title for Jochen Rindt. Emerson and his supporters could scarcely believe their luck.

In 1971 the pace faltered, for he suffered a road accident at Dijon on the way to his new home which he shared with Wilson and their respective wives at Lausanne. His injuries made him miss the Dutch Grand Prix, and only later in the season did he click back into form as Lotus' youthful number one. He was fifth in the Championship and won three Formula 2 races, and then in 1972 there came the flood of success for the disarmingly modest, but intensely competitive and astute Brazilian. To see him 'psyching'

his opponents, and even his team-mates, was a revelation, and he was a young man who had drawn in experience like a magnet; a young man with an old and mature head on his shoulders. . .

Early in 1973 it seemed nothing could go wrong for him. He won the Argentine and Brazilian Grands Prix, the great success in his own back yard at Interlagos sending his countrymen wild with delight, and then he won for the second consecutive year in Spain when his new team-mate, Ronnie Peterson, struck trouble.

It all turned bad in France, where Fittipaldi made an uncharacteristic error in trying to pass new boy Jody Scheckter and triggered a collision which frayed tempers as well as their cars. He retired at Silverstone, and then crashed heavily at Zandvoort when a front wheel broke. He battled grimly against still swollen ankles to take sixth place in Germany. His hopes of retaining his crown faded in Austria, and then vanished in the controversial Italian Grand Prix which Peterson won at Monza.

Fittipaldi was runner-up in the Championship but to his fierce supporters that was not good enough, and it was a rather disgruntled Brazilian who left Lotus at the close of the season and accepted an awful lot of Marlboro-Texaco money to join the McLaren team for 1974.

It was in the modern racing driver

The 1974 World Championship-winning combination — Emerson Fittipaldi and Gordon Coppuck's McLaren M23 design

style of an astute, cool, forward-planning young executive that Fittipaldi took his second World Championship and brought the Constructors' title at last to McLaren. He drove like a tiger to win in Brazil, Belgium and Canada, and stroked his way to points scoring finish after points scoring finish in the other events. In the last race, at Watkins Glen, Clay Regazzoni of Ferrari stood the best chance of pipping him — and he had only won one race. Jody Scheckter of Tyrrell was also in with an outside chance — at least he had won two Grands Prix. In the race that sunny October day, both retired, and Emerson was left to cruise home fourth, as the new World Champion.

He started the 1975 season determined to retain his title. He won in the Argentine, was second in Brazil (to his compatriot Pace) and second again at Monaco. But his political brain was such that he refused to try in a Brands Hatch Race of Champions which admitted what he regarded as dangerous Formula 5000 cars. He qualified 17th on the grid and this petty display of petulance hardly endeared him to the crowd. He atoned for this with a fighting drive at Silverstone where he was beaten by Niki Lauda by just 0·1 second. He walked out of the Spanish GP after a row about unsafe crash barriers (a car did subsequently go into the crowd, although this was not due

to any failing on the part of the barrier). Emerson won the red-flagged British GP by a fluke, but at the end of the year with his crown long gone recovered himself to take two strong second places in Italy and the USA.

Then came the off-season bombshell when he abruptly terminated his McLaren contracts and joined his brother Wilson under the Brazilian Copersucar banner. This national sugar combine reputedly provided the greatest retainer fee ever commanded by a racing driver to attract the ex-World Champion's services, and as the season progressed from bad to worse it seemed that Emerson Fittipaldi was more interested in Swiss francs than in success — despite protestations of patriotic and fraternal loyalty. There was still an exceptional driving talent sheltering within him, however, and he scored three Championship points by finishing in sixth place at Long Beach, Monaco and Brands Hatch. From first to second to 17th in the World Championship table starkly records motor racing's youngest Champion's declining fortunes, but both he and his team were young enough to achieve major success given the right sense of purpose. Despite his fickle tendencies Emerson Fittipaldi was the cleverest and most intellectually skilful of all the early-1970s Grand Prix pilots but he may be remembered as the two-time Champion who lost his way.

Champions

Victory in the perhaps over-publicised World Drivers' Championship depends to an extent on luck, but all the men who follow the Grand Prix circus across the world and who come within striking distance of this title have to be near masters of their trade. The true masters have already been discussed; there are eight other men who have won the Championship once.

Dr Giuseppe 'Nino' Farina

BORN OCTOBER 30, 1908, TURIN, ITALY

This Italian lawyer was already 44 years old in 1950 when he became motor racing's first World Champion Driver. His success exposed the weakness of the Championship, for he won it by a solitary fourth place from Fangio, who was undoubtedly the faster man, but Dr Farina, hard, determined, but very much an Italian gentleman, carried the title worthily.

'Nino' Farina was the son of the eldest of the famous coachbuilding brothers, and nephew of Pinin Farina whose designs have become World famous. He owned and drove his first car, a twin-cylinder Temperino, when he was just nine years old, and while studying law at Turin University he bought an ageing Alfa Romeo 1500 and made his competition debut in the tricky Aosta-Grand St Bernard hill-climb. His father was also competing and finished fourth, while 'Nino' ended the day in hospital with broken bones and a wrecked car. . .

The good Doctor was already enjoying the superiority complex of a wealthy, professional Italian. He had been a brilliant cavalry officer in his military service, and the legend of 'The Great Farina' was already being formed in his own mind when he drove private Maseratis and Alfa Romeos with increasing success in 1933–34.

He was determined to excel, and his

energetic driving broke either the opposition or his car, whichever proved the weaker. His furious style slowly developed and he became one of those rare drivers of national racing in the 1930s whose car was 'alive' all the time. This was one of Nuvolari's tenets for race driving, and the great man took Farina under his wing and coached and advised him. 'Not for one second must your car hang dead', he said, and Farina threw body and soul into emulating the great Mantuan.

In 1934 he won the Masaryk Voiturette GP at Brno; in 1935 he had few successes; in 1936 he joined the

'Nino' Farina graphically explains how his Alfa Romeo is handling to a singularly unimpressed Guidotti — *Capo* of the Italian team and very nearly as good a driver as his Three Fs

Scuderia Ferrari team with Alfa Romeos and was second in the Mille Miglia, following Brivio's car through the night when his own Alfa's lights failed. In 1937 his big 12-cylinder Alfa Romeo won at Naples, and in 1938 Farina became Italian Champion driving for the new works team of *Alfa Corse*. He retained the title in 1939, when Alfa concentrated on Voiturette racing with their new 1½-litre cars and in 1940 he won at Tripoli while the outside world erupted in war.

Already his body was scarred by a long catalogue of racing accidents, including collisions which had killed Marcel Lehoux at Deauville and Laszlo Hartmann at Tripoli, but none served to slow him down. His determination was total, his belief in his own ability unshakable, and his inate skill quite irrefutable. He pushed when others shoved, but he was becoming increasingly tidy as a driver, developing the relaxed straight-arm posture which was to typify him and which many young newcomers were to copy.

After the Second World War, Dr Farina returned to the fray in a works Alfetta, winning the *Grand Prix des Nations* in Geneva in 1946. He drove Maseratis in 1948, proving everywhere with long, beautifully-controlled power slides that The Great Farina had lost none of his touch. That touch handled Maseratis and Ferraris in 1949, and in 1950 *Alfa Corse* set-up the famous 'Three Fs' team with Farina, Fangio and Fagioli as drivers. Farina won at Silverstone, Monza and Berne to take that inaugural World Championship.

He lost his title to his team-mate, Fangio, in 1951 and upon Alfa Romeo's withdrawal he moved to join Ascari and Villoresi at Ferrari. He was unhappy there as Ascari dominated, and his unhappiness often erupted in anger.

This fiery relationship continued, through several spins and crashes and angry scenes, and he was runner-up to Ascari in the Championship. In 1953 he was much more successful in both Formula and sports car races, and he won the German Grand Prix in a tigrish drive sparked by Ascari losing a front wheel while leading. Farina was fourth at the time and he simply blasted past Hawthorn and Fangio to win.

When Ascari went to Lancia, Farina became Ferrari team leader, but he crashed heavily in a 4·9-litre sports car when leading the 1954 Mille Miglia — typically within a few miles of the start, through trying too hard, too soon. Then he was badly burned when his Ferrari threw a half-shaft through its fuel tank during practice for the Monza 1000 Km sports car race.

His sheer grim determination to conquer forced him back into racing in the Argentine in 1955, when despite the need for pain-killing injections he drove hard into second place. He was fourth at Monaco and third in Belgium, but full recovery was a slow process and with the death of Ascari he went into partial retirement, devoting him-

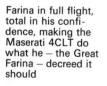

Farina in full flight, total in his confidence, making the Maserati 4CLT do what he — the Great Farina — decreed it should

self to Jaguar distributorships in Italy.

He was still in regular attendance round the circuits, and he made two abortive sorties to Indianapolis, with a Ferrari-engined Kurtis in 1956, and a Kurtis-Offenhauser in 1957 when Keith Andrews crashed it fatally while testing. With this blow, Dr Giuseppe Farina finally retired from racing.

In 1966 the still fit, proud, first World Champion was driving his Lotus-Cortina to the French Grand Prix at Reims when he skidded on an icy road and struck a telegraph pole. The Great Farina, survivor of so many racing accidents was killed. . .

John Michael 'Mike' Hawthorn

BORN APRIL 10, 1929, MEXBOROUGH, YORKSHIRE, ENGLAND

Britain's first World Champion driver, Mike Hawthorn raced for only eight full seasons, and was fully professional in the sense that he was paid to drive for six of them. He won only three Grand Prix races, the Le Mans 24-Hours and a string of minor awards in that time, but he typified the gay, happy-go-lucky characteristics which are expected of the gifted English amateur and carved himself an un-forgettable niche in motor racing history.

Mike Hawthorn was a completely extrovert, beer-drinking, speed happy enthusiast. He loved fast cars and fast motor cycles and raced almost entirely for the fun of it — the fact that he was paid well to enjoy himself was but a minor attraction. He was not an artistic natural driver like Moss, but he was totally fearless, supremely self-confident and on his day could be utterly unbeatable.

His father, Leslie Hawthorn, had been an ace engine tuner, and in 1931 he had moved down from Yorkshire to take over the Tourist Trophy Garage in Farnham, Surrey, to be closer to the Brooklands track.

In 1950 the Hawthorns went racing, running a pair of Rileys, an 1100 cc Imp and a 1500 cc Sprite, in the Brighton Speed Trials. Mike was just 21, and he won his class. The following year Leslie damaged his back and could not drive, so his son ran both Rileys, and won the Ulster and Leinster Trophy races in Ireland in the Sprite, and followed up with the *Motor Sport* Trophy for that season for consistent success in Goodwood meetings.

The burly, blonde young man from Farnham had made quite a name for

himself in these few events, and for 1952 an old friend of the family, Bob Chase, bought him a new 2-litre Cooper-Bristol.

His debut in this car at the Easter Monday Goodwood meeting made headline news. He won his first two races that day and was second in the feature event behind the great Froilan Gonzalez in the $4\frac{1}{2}$-litre Thin Wall Special Ferrari. He led the non Championship Silverstone race until the gear lever broke, and was fourth at Spa in his first Grand Prix. He was third in the British Grand Prix and then third in a Formule Libre race at Bore-

Pals — two good beer drinking British amateurs who just happened to be paid for what they enjoyed doing; Mike Hawthorn seems less amused than his Ferrari co-driver Peter Collins after winning the *Super-cortemaggiore* sports car classic at Monza in 1956

ham in pouring rain which he led for much of the distance against tough works Ferrari opposition.

At the end of the season Enzo Ferrari offered him a drive, and after deep thought Hawthorn accepted that there was no competitive British car, and so joined the Italian team for 1953. He had made up his mind while recovering from a testing crash in the Cooper-Bristol at Modena, and in mid-season he beat Fangio to the line by a second to win the French Grand Prix — the first Englishman to do so since Segrave thirty years before.

This was a euphoric time for the young man from Farnham, although he hated living in Italy and was always

happy to get home from his inevitably hilarious world travels. Then early in 1954 his legs were badly burned in an accident at Syracuse, and British politicians and press began a filthy, vicious campaign against him for not doing his National Service. In fact he was unfit due to a kidney ailment, and the perpetrators of this campaign fully deserved a 'sock in the teeth' which Hawthorn was just the kind of man to give them. He was not a man to brood on such criticism. . .

He was more than man enough to ride such stupidity, but a severe blow to his buoyant spirit came when Leslie Hawthorn crashed his Lancia one night on the way home from Good-

Top: typical Hawthorn on an 'On' day, power-sliding his Squalo Ferrari away from one of the Pedralbes turns on his way to winning the 1954 Spanish Grand Prix. Team-mate Trintignant in the older Ferrari 625 has just made space to let the leader through

Above: tainted victory — Hawthorn in the works D-Type Jaguar at Le Mans in 1955, when his part in the Levegh Mercedes disaster caused International controversy

Champion year — Hawthorn chasing his team-mate Peter Collins during the 1958 British GP. Two weeks later Collins died ahead of Mike at the Nürburgring, and for the first British World Champion it was a bitter title

wood, and was killed. Mike and his father had been very close, and he felt the loss keenly, then came another blow with the death of his boxer dog, which he ran over in his Ferrari when it pranced out to greet him at the Farnham garage . . . that hurt deeply.

The need to manage the garage led him to abandon Ferrari for a British team for 1955, but the Vanwalls he drove needed further development and he returned to the Scuderia in mid-season. Then he was involved in the horrifying Le Mans tragedy in a works Jaguar, and again he suffered at the hands of the Press — the French this time — which held him responsible. Impartial investigation exonerated him completely, but these bitter times had made Hawthorn a harder, rather more cynical man; so he drove harder on circuit, played harder off it, and when the 1956 season with BRM proved another disaster he returned to his first works team — Ferrari.

There he was teamed with his great friend Peter Collins, who was a kindred spirit. He was fourth in the World Championship that year, and in 1958 he beat Moss to the title by just one point to step into Fangio's shoes. He had only won one race to Moss' four, but he had been placed second five times. Sadly the fun was torn out of his racing that season, first by the

death of his team-mate Luigi Musso at Reims and then, savagely, by Collins' fatal crash just ahead of him at the Nürburgring. At this time Mike was bitterly fulfilling his commitments. 'Thank God that's over', he would snarl, 'that's one more race I won't have to do again . . .' It was a bitter, ambivalent attitude, for still on his day he could outdrive them all.

After he had clinched the world title with second place in Morocco, Hawthorn announced his retirement to some public astonishment and much sympathy. He aimed to spend his time with the garage business, and had already spent hours painstakingly restoring his father's 1931 Alfa Romeo 2300 and the famous old Riley, had written a very good autobiography and the 'Carlotti' motor racing boys' stories.

On the morning of January 27, 1959, Mike was driving in his normal, totally fearless manner towards Guildford when he caught and passed Rob Walker — Stirling Moss' entrant. Typically Hawthorn, he grinned and waved two fingers as he hurtled by in his Jaguar saloon, but racing down off the Hogs Back hill he lost control on a wet patch, the Jaguar jack-knifed around a tree, and it was a shattered Rob Walker who found Britain's first World Champion Driver, lying in the wreckage, dead. . .

Philip Toll 'Phil' Hill Jr

BORN APRIL 20, 1927, MIAMI, FLORIDA, USA

America's first World Champion was a terrific sports car driver, a useful Grand Prix driver, a good engineer, and one of the few totally honest men ever to achieve fame in motor racing. Like Mike Hawthorn he was a motor car enthusiast; he knew them, he loved them, and he drove them fast with sympathy.

Hill's father was postmaster of Santa Monica, California, and Phil's early passion was for automobiles. He was orphaned when quite young, and this made him a rather withdrawn, quiet character, although in his later years — when described as highly-strung and excitable — that very description was one of the few things liable to light his fuse.

He studied business administration at university, but his fascination for motor cars finally found him working as a mechanic, and proud owner of an MG TC which at that time was the prize of every young Californian male. He drove the car to his first race win at Carrell Speedway, Los Angeles in 1948, and the following year found him in England, studying in the service

departments of SU Carburettors, Jaguar and Rolls-Royce.

He took home with him a Jaguar XK120, and in 1950 he drove it to win his first road race, at Pebble Beach on Monterey Peninsula. Like his English namesake, he worked as a mechanic in return for sponsored drives, and in 1952 Allen Guiberson entered him in a Ferrari in the mighty *Carrera Panamericana* race through Mexico. He finished sixth. In 1953 in Mexico, he and his passenger, Richie Ginther, were lucky to survive a colossal accident. Phil talked of retiring, but drove an OSCA at Le Mans and returned to Mexico in 1954 where he placed second, again with Ginther in the passenger seat.

Ferrari invited him to Le Mans in 1955, through Luigi Chinetti their American distributor, but the disaster there following so closely on Bill Vukovich's fiery and much-publicised death at Indianapolis persuaded him once more to retire from driving.

But in December he returned, to win at Nassau, and Chinetti then arranged for him to share a works Ferrari with Olivier Gendebien in the Argentine 1 000 km race the following month. The pair placed second, and an invita-

tion came from Maranello to join the works team.

So Phil Hill arrived in Modena, and became a fully-fledged works Ferrari driver. For two years he was retained as a sports car and test driver, and was very successful as such — he became the first American ever to win Le Mans — but he was beginning to feel a Formula 1 chance would never come when he was third in the 500-Miles track race at Monza and then drove Jo Bonnier's private Maserati 250F in the French Grand Prix at Reims. He finished seventh, and in recognition was given his Ferrari Formula 1 debut in the Italian Grand Prix, which he led and eventually finished in third place. In Morocco he set the pace, then shut off to allow Hawthorn to take his World Championship. A new star had been born.

In 1959 Phil Hill found his Grand Prix feet, and in 1960 he won the Italian Grand Prix in one of the ageing front-engined Ferraris, in the absence of the British works teams. He was the first American *Grande Epreuve* winner since Murphy in 1921.

The following season Ferrari had an advantage with their new V6 1½-litre engines, but the chassis hardly

Sweet joy of success — Phil Hill (right) celebrates his 1962 Le Mans victory with co-driver Olivier Gendebien. It was the last of the intelligent Californian's three 24-Hour victories, and the last of the aristocratic Belgian's four

Below, left: the final flag sweeps down on Phil Hill's honourable career as the Chaparral 2F which he shared with Mike Spence rumbles across the Brands Hatch finish line to win the 1967 BOAC 500

Phil Hill made his single-seater reputation in the tricky Ferrari Dino 246s. Here at Silverstone he fights the good fight against his namesake, Graham, in the BRM, with teammate von Trips and Ireland's Lotus following

matched and although the Italian team had a performance advantage, Hill, von Trips and Richie Ginther had to fight all the way. This the frantically gum-chewing Hill and the urbane Trips did to good effect. Phil won at Spa, and the Championship lay between them in the Italian Grand Prix, with 33 points to Trips and 29 to the American. Hill led all the way, while poor Trips crashed fatally on the second lap. The straight-forward, quiet American became a grief-stricken World Champion. . .

During 1962, when he won his third Le Mans race with Gendebien the new Champion struggled with Ferrari Formula 1 cars which were already over the hill. After a scintillating, fighting drive for second place at Monaco, things went from bad to worse, and at the end of the year Phil Hill and Ferrari parted company.

He went to the new ATS team, which had a disastrous 1963 season. He drove sports cars for Porsche, and in 1964 appeared in Coopers before crashing two in Austria and leaving the team under a cloud, then being re-called for the American races.

Nothing was going right for the stocky Californian, and in 1965 he was absent from the World Championship races, and forged an association with Jim Hall's Chaparral team instead. In 1966 he shared the radical Chaparral 2D coupe with Bonnier to win the Nürburgring 1 000 km race, he won a CanAm round in the winged 2E and then returned to Europe in 1967 with the giant 2F winged coupe. He shared with Mike Spence to win the BOAC Six Hours race at Brands Hatch on July 30, and then quietly retired with that good victory to his name.

John Surtees

BORN FEBRUARY 11, 1934, TATSFIELD, KENT, ENGLAND

Determined, outspoken, totally dedi-cated, a brilliant motor cyclist, one of the fastest racing drivers of his day; this was John Surtees — the only man to become World Champion on both two wheels and four.

His father, Jack Surtees, was an effective motor cyclist and a garage proprietor in Kent, and John was proud owner of his first motor cycle at 11. On leaving school at 15 he went straight into the garage business as a mechanic, and in 1950 made his competition debut as sidecar pas-senger to his father. In 1951 he made his solo debut on a grass track at Luton. He won his first race, at Brands Hatch, at 17, and by 1955 he had beaten the great Geoff Duke, had won 68 out of 76 races in that season alone, and was offered a works MV Agusta ride for 1956. He ended the year as 500 cc Champion of the World, and he added six more world titles to his tally by the end of 1959.

The Italians doted on him. He be-came *Il Grande John* to their sporting press, and when he turned to racing on four wheels in 1960 the English mistranslated 'John the Great' into

John Surtees — the only World Cham-pion on both two and four wheels since the Champion-ship series began

'Big John', and the name stuck.

Early in 1960, although still con-tracted to MV, Surtees was lapping Goodwood in a Vanwall, learning how to handle a racing car, and making his mistakes, in private. In between spins

he clipped nearly two seconds off the unofficial lap record. On March 18 Ken Tyrrell gave him his debut drive in a Formula Junior Cooper, and he placed second to another budding youngster named Jim Clark. At Silverstone on May 14 Surtees made his Formula 1 debut in a Lotus, and when his two-wheeled commitments allowed, he drove for Colin Chapman's team for the rest of the season.

He staggered the establishment by finishing second in the British Grand Prix, and in Portugal he started from pole and led before crashing mildly. He was pushing himself and his car to find how both would react in this strange kind of racing, and sometimes his lightning reflexes were not enough to retrieve some ticklish situations — he spun and crashed and was visibly on the ragged edge most of the time.

In 1961 he left motor cycling to concentrate on cars, but his Yeoman Credit team Coopers were sub-standard and after two early minor wins he picked up only four Championship points. He tied with Jack Brabham, but that did not satisfy him at all.

For the new year he wanted his own car which he himself could test and develop. Eric Broadley of Lola built it, and by mid-season Surtees was a front runner. This kind of operation satisfied this introspective, rather suspicious man's sense of independence, but after taking fourth place in the Championship he was on the move again. Ferrari beckoned him with a three-year contract, and in those seasons he was to work among Italians once more whose enormous respect he returned by beginning to win.

His first success was at the Nürburgring, and he won non-Championship races at Enna and Kyalami plus a string of sports car classics. Sensitive, cool and determined, his driving had matured greatly during his first year with Ferrari, and when they gave him new equipment for 1964 he rose to the occasion and stole the Championship on the very last lap of the Mexican Grand Prix after a late-season charge.

By this time he had a great reputation as a searching test driver and self-taught development engineer, and his

John Surtees hurls
his Surtees TS7
through the Karussel
at the Nürburgring
in 1971.

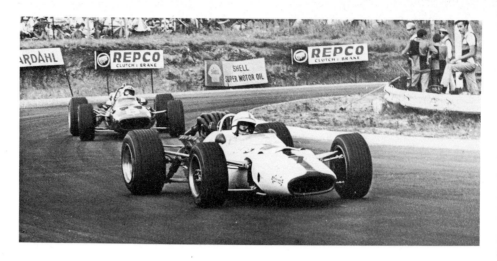

Having seen what Honda did to the motor-cycle racing World, the Japanese concern seemed a good bet for Formula 1 in 1967–68. Surtees' Honda hopes usually went up in smoke, but here at Kyalami in 1968 the car appears to be running strongly ahead of Chris Amon's Ferrari

First CanAm Champion – Surtees' 1966 exploits with his own Lola-Chevrolet T70 earned him rich prize money and a worthy place in the record books

total dedication both at the wheel and behind the scenes was paying rich dividends. But during 1965 pressures began to mount within the Ferrari team as Lorenzo Bandini perhaps got better machinery than befitted a 'number two', team manager Dragoni favoured Bandini at Surtees' expense and meanwhile the Englishman was working closely with Eric Broadley on the Lola T70 sports car programme, and with Lola Formula 2s. Despite his unusually close accord with *Commendatore* Ferrari these activities were frowned upon. He should not be risking injury in other cars.

At Mosport he crashed heavily in his T70, suffering severe injuries, but

the winter saw him stage a near miraculous recovery to race and win again for Ferrari in the Monza 1000 Km in April, 1966. The new 3-litre Ferrari was the first new Formula 1 car to appear that year, and Surtees won brilliantly at Spa in pouring rain before differences with Dragoni came to a head and he left the team abruptly at Le Mans.

Cooper took him on, and he developed their heavy Maserati-engined cars into competitive prospects and won the last race of the year in Mexico. For 1967 he moved to Honda, whom he had seen rise to dominate the motor-cycling World. They were not to do the same in Formula 1, and only

when he adopted a Lola chassis late in the year did he win a dramatic Italian Grand Prix.

Honda Racing was very much a Surtees team, based in Slough and run totally by the man himself. He was never a man to delegate anything he felt he could do better himself, and his increasing involvement with administration as well as design, development and driving seemed to take the edge off his track performance.

When Honda withdrew at the close of 1968, Surtees moved to BRM, who needed his development and 'team doctor' skills if ever a team did. But they were hopeless, and Surtees spent more and more time in his own company, building and entering Formula 5000 cars under the Team Surtees name. Here, where he could be team proprietor, manager, driver, admini-strator, even mechanic, he was at last content, and in 1970 he introduced his own Formula 1 Surtees TS7, and he used the car and its successors to win two Oulton Park Gold Cup races although Grand Prix success remained elusive. By 1972 'Big John' had phased himself out of driving, and made a lone appearance in the Italian Grand Prix just to race-develop his latest TS14 car.

By this time he had others doing the driving for him, although he still tested and developed his cars himself. But although Mike Hailwood won the Formula 2 Championship in Surtees cars the old magic seemed long gone, and Formula 1 successes have proved sparse. By 1975 the Champion days were long, long gone and Surtees cars a perennial also-ran reminder of largely unfulfilled potential.

Following pages: Denny Hulme's Repco Brabham BT24 clears the old 12·8km 'yump' at the Nürburgring on his way to winning the 1967 German GP. His Championship win that season gave him a crown which rested uncomfortably

Denis Clive 'Denny' Hulme

BORN JUNE 18, 1936, MOTUEKA, SOUTH ISLAND, NEW ZEALAND

Ken Tyrrell wanted a Formula Junior driver for 1963. He had thought of several and discounted them when someone suggested Denny Hulme, a rugged New Zealander with a rather remote manner but a promising record. Tyrrell discounted him as well; 'He's too fat and lazy to be any good . . .' Four years later Denny was World Champion . . . and he had put himself there by sheer grit and hard work.

Denny had been born on a small dairy farm in the tobacco growing area of Motueka. His father won a wartime VC for gallantry in Crete, and when invalided home he bought a small trucking business in the seaside village of Pongakawa, just outside the township of Te Puke. There Denny grew up with the sun, the sea and the guts of trucks, and in his late-'teens he was enthralled by a chance drive in an MG TF. He put so much work into the business that his father, Clive, bought him a new TF as a gift, and when some friends prompted him into showing it off he tried a club hill-climb and knocked six seconds off the class record. From that point on there was no turning back.

Denny Hulme in more of a teddy bear mood than his usual grizzly bear mien. The New Zealander won here at Monza in 1969

101

For 1958 he raced an MGA, and after the New Zealand GP at Ardmore he bought a 2-litre Cooper-Climax, a real single-seater. With that car he earned a 'Driver to Europe' scholarship, tying with George Lawton, and the pair of them were despatched to Britain early in 1960. Bruce McLaren had won the same trip two years previously, and now he was a works Cooper Grand Prix driver. That season was marred by George Lawton's fatal crash at Roskilde in Denmark, but Denny drove Coopers in Formula Junior, Formula 2 and in Formula 1, where he made a brief debut at Snetterton.

While preparing his own cars, as Bruce had before him, in Cooper's pokey works at Surbiton, Hulme did a deal with Reg Parnell to take a 2½-litre car back home with him. He returned triumphantly, and took the National Gold Star as had McLaren after his first season abroad.

The next two seasons were dismal, as Denny's natural reserve prevented him knocking on doors to sell his services. It was all hard work as he led a gypsy life round Europe, then took a job in a Brabham garage.

Jack's manager, Phil Kerr, knew the rugged Hulme from their native New Zealand, and he could see his potential but Brabham could not. Right at the end of the 1962 season their works Junior driver broke his collarbone,

Denny won the drive and proved his point, to gain a regular works ride for 1963. He won seven of his 14 races that year, and had a Formula 1 ride at Karlskoga in Sweden.

He was elevated to the new Formula 2 team for the following season and proved himself an admirable number two to 'Black Jack'. On occasion he could look just as black himself, and his car was just as sideways, just as fast as the Guv'nor's. In 1965 he had his first Grand Prix rides as Jack began to stand aside, and in 1966 and 1967 he was Brabham's regular number two, now capable of running with the best opposition, and of winning.

In the 1967 season he won the Monaco and German Grands Prix, and picked up sufficient places to clinch the title in Mexico simply by following his team leader home. That season also saw him bursting onto the American scene, finishing fourth at Indianapolis in a private Eagle to be voted 'Rookie of the Year' and helping Bruce McLaren to dominate CanAm in the Kiwi team's sports cars.

Denny's World Championship was an irksome title. 'The worst thing in the world is making speeches', he complained, and he later admitted he just was not ready to take full advantage of the doors that his title could have opened to him. As it was, he did not enjoy the title, he did not cash in on it, and when he moved to McLaren for

Paying the rent — Hulme in the 1970 McLaren-Chevrolet M8D at the Laguna Seca CanAm round in California. He and Bruce McLaren dominated this lucrative Championship from 1967–70, alternating as CanAm Champions until Bruce's untimely death

Debut of a classic racing car – Denny started the 1973 South African GP from pole position in the McLaren M23 prototype and looked set to win before a puncture delayed his progress

Formula 1 and CanAm racing in 1968 although he fought to retain it into the last round, perhaps – sneakingly – he just might have been a little happy when he lost it.

He won the CanAm Championship and two Grands Prix that season, was fourth again at Indianapolis and became motor racing's top International dollar earner on sheer winnings, while in 1969 he picked up another Formula 1 victory in the Mexican race and played second fiddle in CanAm, as it was Bruce's 'turn'.

The two New Zealanders were firm friends, McLaren being the more outgoing, the natural public figure, while Hulme was more withdrawn, more irascible, but an easy-going man who knew his job to the 'Nth' degree and who could talk easily about it if he felt the person he was talking to genuinely wanted to know and was 'his kind of bloke'.

In pre-'500' testing at Indianapolis Denny was badly burned when his new McLaren caught fire, and for days there was a danger that he might lose some fingers. He bore the agony with craggy calm, but three weeks later when Bruce was killed he broke down in his grief. Bruce had been the engineer-driver and Denny the racing driver in their team; their relationship had grown over the years – now it had been chillingly ripped apart.

Hulme fought his way back into

Following pages:
Emerson Fittipaldi in brother Wilson's Copersucar attacked the 1977 season with more hope than confidence

racing some five weeks after the Indy fire, and immediately placed third in the CanAm race at Mosport with his injured and still bandaged fingers shaped to fit the big car's steering wheel. By the end of the season he had won the CanAm title again, 'for Bruce', and he figured mightily in the McLaren Racing survival programme which brought him more Formula 1 and CanAm success into 1974. By that time he had long decided that this season was to be his last as a driver, and close contact with the aftermath of accidents which killed Francois Cevert and his former team-mate, Peter Revson, persuaded him to drive well within his true capabilities in those last few races. In these late years he was more craggy, more irascible, more 'Denny the Bear' than ever before, but he was consistently under-rated and even at eight-tenths his lap times were fast and competitive amongst a contemporary horde of indifferent GP drivers.

When he retired at the end of the season Denny was looking forward to returning to his native New Zealand, enjoying his family, returning to the sea-shore and the sun, and the prospect of not really having to work hard again. He was that kind of man, an intensely private person, a man who shunned the public and publicity but a man who in fact had more supporters than perhaps he ever knew. . .

Karl Jochen Rindt

BORN AUGUST 18, 1942, MAINZ, GERMANY

To become motor racing's first post-humous World Champion was a tragic fate for this great natural driver. During 1969 and 1970 he was the only man who could match his great friend Jackie Stewart car for car, while his total determination, uncanny car control and supreme bravery had made him king of Formula 2 since 1967.

He had been orphaned when 15-months old in an Allied bombing raid on Hamburg, and like so many Germans of that tragic generation he grew up parentless, wild, aggressive, totally self-possessed to the point of boorishness, and imbued with an unconcerned will to win whatever he was doing.

Rindt was brought up in Graz in southern Austria, under the guardianship of his grandfather Dr Hugo Martinowitz, who was a solicitor. Jochen was a moneyed young man when he came of age, the capital from the family spice mill company of Klein & Rindt having been administered by his guardians.

As a boy he ran wild around Graz, hopeless academically but excellent at ball-games and skiing. At 15 he was conning rides on moped cycles, and he charged around in a few moto-cross events before being packed off to England to learn the language.

He was sent to Chichester, and while there he saw his first race meeting at Goodwood. It did not appeal, until he was back in Graz, was 18 years old and driving his own Simca Montlhéry. He entered for a race at Innsbruck, and finished third. In 1962 he invested in an Alfa Romeo Giulietta TI, and gained more racing experience at the expense of his studies at Vienna Polytechnic for World Trade, and for the following year he bought a Formula Junior Cooper. He made his debut in that car at Vallelunga, outside Rome, and qualified on pole position, and then won his next race. So his career blossomed, initially as a carefree wealthy amateur, trailing around Europe in an E-Type Jaguar and frightening the life out of his opposition! The 1963 Austrian GP at

Zeltweg saw him racing against Clark and Brabham with a 1500 cc Ford engine in the Cooper. It threw a rod.

He won some backing from Ford Austria for the 1964 season and bought a brand-new Formula 2 Brabham with which he staggered British enthusiasts by arriving out of the blue at Mallory Park and then the Crystal Palace circuit and promptly winning the latter race outright from Graham Hill. The impossible way he hurled his car into the corners at all angles proved possible as he left them with his foot hard down, and the car snaking to fight free of his control. If he survived he was going to win. He was good enough to survive, and repeated such antics lap after lap.

Rob Walker gave him his Formula 1 debut in the Austrian Grand Prix at Zeltweg but he retired his Brabham when the steering started to fall apart, and at the close of the year he signed a three-season contract with Cooper.

They were well into their decline at this time, and he was to have a sorry time with them, hampered by his machinery. He compensated by sharing a lucky win at Le Mans in that first 1965 season with Masten Gregory, in a private Ferrari, and then he went Formula 2 racing with the Winkelmann Brabham team and rose to dominate

Jochen Rindt celebrates his first Grand Prix victory at Watkins Glen in 1969. Piers Courage, standing alongside, was second in this race. In 1970 both died in Formula 1 accidents — the Austrian becoming the sport's first post-humous World Champion, and hopefully the last

Above: where Rindt was king — Formula 2 racing, exemplified here at Thruxton in 1970 with the Austrian's own Lotus 69 leading Jackie Stewart's John Coombs-entered Brabham

Rindt's prowess with the heavy and unweildy Cooper-Maseratis finally marked him down as a man to watch during 1966, when his fearless style and natural skills shone brightly — despite the car

the class with total assurance.

His Formula 2 outings were a better yardstick for his ability than his battles, however heroic, with the Formula 1 Coopers, and it was logical in 1968 that he should join Jack Brabham in the works Grand Prix team. Brabham, Tauranac and Rindt got on very well together. They were all men who spoke their minds fearlessly and it was only the wretched unreliability of their quad-cam Repco engines which kept Rindt out of the results.

Perhaps his greatest drive was in the 1968 French GP practice at Rouen, for which he qualified on pole position in a shattering performance, only to be put out of the race by a fuel leak. In

Left: first victory for James Hunt came at Zandvoort in 1975 when he outfumbled the might of Ferrari in his Hesketh 308B

Below: Jackie Stewart scored a record-breaking 27 Championship-qualifying GP victories in his career. Here at Monaco in 1971 he won one of his hardest, for Tyrrell 003 started the race with its rear brakes virtually inoperative

Right: Niki Lauda's Ferrari 312T2 leads the pack down towards the old station hairpin at Monaco in 1976. He scored an untroubled win, but near-disaster later in the year at the Nürburgring robbed him of his Championship title

Germany the Repco-Brabham kept going to power him through the murk into a brave third place.

Brabham could not keep him, although they wanted him dearly and Jochen too wanted to stay but knew he could receive better money, and a better chance, with Lotus. The money was extremely important to him . . . he never forgot his own value.

Even so, he moved reluctantly from Brabham's, and in 1969 had a season of great battles with Stewart, or spins and crashes and for much of the year victory still eluded him. He had a monstrous accident at Barcelona when his car's wing failed, but after recovering from facial injuries he won his very next race, in Formula 2 at Zolder.

Jochen had been in Grand Prix racing for four and a half seasons without a win when he went to Watkins Glen and scored that long awaited maiden victory, in the United States Grand Prix. 'Typical Jochen', said his friends, 'waits for the richest race of the year . . .'

Now winning was to become a habit, and in 1970 he won with the aid of large slices of luck at Monaco, Brands Hatch, and Clermont-Ferrand,

and by out-driving the opposition at Zandvoort and Hockenheim.

He could have won the Championship on his home ground in Austria, but his Lotus 72 suffered an engine failure. Then came Monza, and practice for the Italian Grand Prix. Trying for too fast a time, with the wing incidence freshly reduced, and new, unscrubbed tyres, Rindt tried perhaps too hard, or perhaps something broke in his car. It bulleted into the Armco barrier on the 170 mph entry to the Curva Parabolica, slammed under it into a lamp stanchion and pirouetted back with its entire front half smashed away. If Jochen was not dead already there was no hope of his surviving terrible chest and leg injuries, and officially he died in the ambulance on the way to a Milan hospital.

Jochen left a wife, Nina, and a small daughter. He had promised that he would retire if he won the World Championship, but he did not have that chance. In many ways it was ironic that Fittipaldi won the United States Grand Prix to deprive Jacky Ickx of nine title points, and so posthumously fulfil the Austrian ace's ambition . . .

Prelude to near-disaster at Barcelona in 1969 as Rindt's Lotus 49 rear wing begins to buckle under stress. Within minutes it collapsed and hurled the car into a very high-speed accident which the Austrian was immensely fortunate to survive. Graham Hill's sister car had suffered a carbon-copy failure moments earlier

Nikolaus-Andreas 'Niki' Lauda

BORN FEBRUARY 22, 1949, VIENNA, AUSTRIA

After the retirement of Jackie Stewart at the end of the 1973 season followers of motor racing waited to see who would emerge as the new standard-setter; the man to take Stewart's crown as the fastest driver of his time. Ronnie Peterson had stolen some of the Scot's glory during that final careful season,

wealthy paper-processing plant owner in Vienna. He began driving early, an indispensable background for the great racing driver, and was only ten or eleven years old as he trundled about the paper works' yard in various BMWs, Opels, VWs and the occasional half-ton truck. When nobody

Niki Lauda — a thirsty 'Mouse' supporting his sponsor, Romerquelle health drink, after practice at the Nürburgring, 1976. The following day the reigning World Champion had apparently 'psyched' himself into an accident, and was fighting for his life in a clinical burns unit

and then in 1974 the mercurial Swede lost his talisman — the Player Lotus cars foundered — and Niki Lauda 'clicked' for Ferrari.

During the 1974 season the slightly-built, youthful-looking Austrian placed his Ferrari on pole position for nine of the year's 15 Championship grands prix, led eight of them and won two. He was consistently the fastest of a typical season after a Champion has retired in which those who were left fought to assume his supremacy. In 1975 the picture was more complete, as Lauda again took nine pole positions but in a 14-race Grand Prix season, and won five of them to become World Champion Driver. Into 1976 he was the top of the pile, and it took a horrifying accident in the German Grand Prix to knock him off his perch, despite a winning battle for his life and for his continued career which won the World's heart.

Niki Lauda was born the son of a

was looking he also tended to drive them out through the gates, and take himself for a quiet jaunt on the public road.

As yet he had little or no interest in what was to become his sport, and it was not until the late-1960s that he saw his first motor race, accompanying a cousin to the Nürburgring. He was hooked by what he saw and within a few weeks was hill-climbing his own VW saloon in Austrian club events. In July, 1968, he borrowed some cash from his two grandmothers — supposedly to buy some land — and quietly invested in a Porsche 911S to go up a class in his hill-climbing. Father eventually heard of his son's activities and the family were outraged, yet Niki somehow managed to appear in Formula Vee single-seater racing in 1969, at the wheel of a Kaimann. During that year he had twenty races in the car, won eight of them, was second in six more and third three times. One of his

Above, left: while struggling to learn the ropes in Formula 1, Lauda won the minor British Formula 2 Championship and had some good European outings in this March 712

second places came on his debut in the car, at Hockenheim in April, and by the end of the season his natural talents were making him a man to watch.

For 1970 he arranged a deal with the German-domiciled American constructor Francis McNamara to buy one of his spaceframe Formula 3 cars at half-price. Highlights of the year were a desperately hard-fought second place at Brno in Czechoslovakia, where he virtually dead-heated on the finish line with the quick Swiss driver, Jurg Dubler. Such a result in that kind of Formula 3 company augured well for the Viennese, and he followed it up with a fourth at Zandvoort and led at Knutsdorp in Sweden. Then came a Belgian event at Zolder, and there he crashed heavily while avoiding an ambulance crossing the track, and the McNamara was completely written-off. It was not to be rebuilt.

Lauda escaped from that almighty accident virtually unharmed, and for the latter part of the season decided to try his hand in sports car racing. His single-seater exploits had attracted backing from Bosch, the German automotive electrical company, and with added assistance from his father (now converted to his son's interests) Niki bought a 3-litre Porsche 908.

With this potent car he won at Osterreichring, was third at the Nürburgring and fourth at Thruxton on a visit to England. Fifth places fell to the Lauda 908 at Imola and on the Norisring street circuit at Nuremburg, then came sixth place in the World Championship of Makes 1000 km race at Osterreichring, where he shared his car with the oddly-named Peter Peter.

With some parental support the toothy Viennese arranged sufficient backing from the *Erste Osterreichische Sparkasse* bank to join the precariously-financed March 'renta drive' F2 team for 1971. At the Nürburgring in May he showed promise of things to come by battling with veteran drivers Graham Hill and Peter Westbury for fourth place behind

In 1974 Niki Lauda was instrumental in bringing Ferrari back to the fore as a Grand Prix force to be reckoned with. Here at Jarama he leads team-mate Regazzoni on the way to his first Grand Prix victory

Francois Cevert, Emerson Fittipaldi and Carlos Reutemann. Lauda lost when a wishbone broke.

It was at Rouen that the fast-improving newcomer made his mark, by wrenching first place in the first heat away from his team leader — Ronnie Peterson! In those days *nobody* led Ronnie in Formula 2 if his car was healthy, and vigorous pit-signalling was necessary to restore team order before the finish — when Niki again 'had a go' on the last lap but was just pipped to the post. In the final that day he finished fourth.

In September he ran second at Albi before another wishbone broke, and at the end of the season he had a considerable store of hard-won experience to accompany tenth place in the European Formula 2 Championship. He had also made his Formula 1 debut as the bank hired him the spare works March 711 for the Austrian GP. The car 'was lousy . . .'

Niki's motor racing ambitions were becoming too serious for his family. It

seemed that they had wanted him to get it out of his system, and instead he had become hooked. He felt that March were the best Formula 1 team to accommodate a novice and with the bank as sponsor had arranged a £35000 deal to drive a second car for the 1972 season. His family contacted the bank and stopped the deal. Niki found himself with a contract and no money of his own to fulfil it now that his sponsor had been warned off. Boldly he arranged with another bank, the *Raiffeisenkasse* to loan him the money over five years. He offered to wear their decals on his helmet and they agreed to make the loan interest free.

During that first Grand Prix season Niki Lauda looked utterly out of his depth after a brief sparkle in South Africa where he finished seventh behind Graham Hill's Brabham. Part of the trouble was the undriveability of March's 721X, followed by the lack of development time in which to sort out the replacement 721G. Ronnie Peterson's experience and animal skill made the most of his number one team position to turn the 721G into a potent contender by the end of the year, but Lauda's car was never sorted to the same degree. Some small consolation came in Formula 2 in which he won the minor British National Championship for the March team.

Still he owed something like £30000 of his *Raiffeisenkasse* loan, and the Marlboro money man, Patrick Duffeler, came up with a deal whereby Niki joined BRM for 1972 more or less on merit, but without a retainer. He joined Clay Regazzoni and Jean-Pierre Beltoise as very much the team number three. In Belgium he was fifth to score his first Championship points and at Monte Carlo he stormed into a fighting third place only for his car to break. After that performance Louis Stanley, BRM's autocratic director, offered him a new contract with the opportunity to earn some money. Despite Lauda's background he needed desperately to earn money. He still had the bank loan to pay off.

In Britain Niki led from the restart but briefly, and back at the Nürburgring

Champion duo – Niki Lauda and the 1975 Ferrari 312T; the smoothest, neatest and quickest combination around

again excelled, out-qualified his experienced team-mates and was fourth for a lap before crashing heavily when his BRM broke. He broke a small bone in his hand, missed his own GP at Osterreichring, and made a comeback at Monza where he crashed again — without consequence.

Niki had always maintained that the BRM chassis handled as well as any, but that it lacked the power and the team organisation to back it up. In the wet Canadian GP he proved something about the car and his own prowess by running away in the lead until the rain eased, the track dried and he had to change tyres. A broken crownwheel finally ended his most promising day yet. But he was unhappy at the high-handed way in which Stanley had dropped Regazzoni from the team for that race, and with offers from Maranello to join Ferrari the young Austrian knew where he was going for 1974.

After the shambolic organisation of BRM, Lauda found Ferrari a team having one of their periodic upswings. They had dropped their sports car programme and at Fiat's bidding were concentrating purely on their Formula 1 commitments. With his ex-BRM team-mate Regazzoni, Lauda quickly snapped into gear in the revised 312B3 cars, and first time out in the Argentine Niki placed second behind Denny Hulme's McLaren with Regga third on his tail. In Spain, to start the European season, the Ferrari pair finished 1—2 with Lauda scoring his first *Grande Epreuve* victory. He was second in Belgium, won again in Holland, was second in France, and was leading the World Championship at Brands Hatch for the British GP. He was leading clearly when a tyre was damaged on crash debris and slowly deflated. His relative immaturity showed as he refused to come in to change the tyre, and left his inevitable stop so late he had no chance of recovery. As it was the tyre shredded, he corkscrewed into his pit on the penultimate lap, and the organisers had allowed the end of the pit road to be choked with hangers-on and even a course car. He was credited with ninth place after abandoning his car, close to tears, before the jam. Ferrari appealed to the FIA and they awarded Lauda a notional fifth place and two more Championship points which he had not scored. It was the beginning of the end that season.

Tweaked-up at the Nürburging he started from pole position after a shattering practice performance, got off the line badly and crashed at the second corner . . . trying too hard too soon. It was immaturity again. There could be no excuses. In Austria he ran second before the Ferrari failed him, and at Monza he led before it failed again. The partisan crowd booed and jeered Ferrari in general and the Austrian in particular. A savage anti-Lauda campaign was launched in the Italian 'sporting' press. He was not trying,

The Mouse Returns — Lauda's victory in the 1977 South African GP was a copybook success. He simply drove away from the best the opposition could offer, nursing his ailing Ferrari through the closing laps with debris from Pryce's crashed Shadow still jammed under the 312T2

they said. He was breaking his cars, they said. An Italian-born driver should drive for Ferrari, they said . . . but there was not one of Niki's class. . .

Last chance of redemption was in Canada, and there another error of judgement which allowed drivers ahead of him to negotiate dust and debris thrown onto the track by an accident while he lost control of his car and crashed himself put paid to his Championship hopes.

Lauda's performances had injected new life into the whole Ferrari team which was now moulded around him and around their executive-in-the-field, the youthful *Marchese* Luca di Montezemolo. In 1975 they set the record straight and Niki won five Grand Prix races, three consecutively, to clinch his World Championship crown. He added to these laurels the International Trophy race at Silverstone and went into 1976 determined to retain his title.

The old worries of the bank loan repayments were now far behind him. He was a big-money superstar — as much as any Ferrari man ever could be — but typically it showed in his track achievement rather than money-making but time-wasting fringe activities. He was like a virtuoso musician who practised his instrument until he could produce an unmatchable performance. He seemed to have whittled away at his own abilities until he had tuned-out the occasional lapses, the immaturity, and his driving

was smooth, unspectacular, he did not bounce over kerbs, did not abuse his car. Some 'experts' who should have known better put down his success airily to '40 more horsepower' because he was so unspectacular. They were blinded by their own idea of superstar behaviour. They called Lauda 'The Rat' because of his unfortunate rodent visage and his undisguised contempt for the mediamen. Others more objective thought of him as 'The Mouse' — free of malice, a little devious, highly-skilled; laughing all the way to the bank while the mediamen twisted their vitriolic knives in an attempt to put down the Viennese gentleman who had given perfectly stupid answers, or no answer at all, to their perfectly stupid questions. . .

In the new season Ferrari won the first six rounds of the World Championship, five falling to Lauda, one to Regazzoni. But it was not that simple, for in Spain 'The Mouse' drove with cracked ribs and feeling decidedly groggy after turning a tractor over on himself at his Salzburg estate. He could not stand the pace, settled back to let the competition flood by, then pulled himself together and charged home second behind Hunt's McLaren. That car was subsequently disqualified, and Lauda instated as the winner. Then the counter-protests and appeals began which were to mar a ridiculous season, and in the British GP he was beaten fair-and-square by Hunt in the re-run after probably being the cause

117

of a collision which caused the first race to be red-flagged. His gearbox played up during the race but he finished second and then the Ferrari lawyers justifiably began yet more legal drama to remove Hunt from the results and give Niki the victory.

In Germany Lauda was tense and nervous. Despite his previous fine performances at the 'Ring he was frightened of it, and did not mind admitting so. As a married and big-money earning man he seemed to be bowing beneath new responsibilities. Safety had always bothered him, he even admitted he had originally painted his helmet dayglo red so that rescuers could find him should he be thrown out amongst the trees and bushes somewhere like the 'Ring or Brno . . . and he was not smiling that wan smile when he said that. Now his misgivings about the 'Ring seemed to psych him into the mother and father of fiery accidents, as he uncharacteristically misjudged a curve before Bergwerk Corner, jounced over a high kerb, careered through catch-fences to strike a bank backwards and then ricocheted to a halt with the car gutted by catch-fence poles and burning furiously.

He was dragged from the fire by other drivers and a marshal, and was in a critical condition for several days with lungs apparently damaged by flame and toxic smoke inhalation. On the second night he was horrified to find a priest giving him absolution. He metaphorically leaped from his bed and began doing press-ups. That seems to have been the turning point, and despite severe burn damage to his right ear and around his eyes he battled his way back from death's door. His pulmonary injuries were found to be less severe than first feared, and to universal astonishment and admiration he reappeared on the Monza grid for the Italian Grand Prix!

It was the same story as 1973, when he had crashed and hurt himself at the Nürburgring at the start of August, and was back at Monza at the start of September. That time he had broken his hand. This time he had been burned within an inch of his life.

Would it be the same 'Mouse'.

Practice proved it was. The swift, cold, pale blue eyes summoned team manager, engineer and mechanics as he made his pit stops. A brisk fore-finger signalled what he required. In the race Niki Lauda finished fourth, exhausted but still in the World Championship lead. The Monza fans who had jeered in 1974 and cheered in 1975 massed in the finish area to greet Ronnie Peterson the GP winner, then Regazzoni who had been second for Ferrari. Someone began to chant 'Lauda, Lauda' — others took it up — 'LauDA, LaUDA, LAUDAAAH'. The little man was too bushed to appear, it was not his style in any case, but he could hear them . . . he had done something in the Nuvolari mould.

But thereafter the year went bad again. Ferrari had lost their test and development tempo, in Canada hasty changes were made to the cars in a desperate attempt to make the latest batch of Goodyear tyres work on their chassis and the modified pick-up points broke. Niki dropped from a possible fifth place to eighth, out of the points. In the USA he awoke his rival James Hunt on race morning and announced 'Today I vill be World Champion'. Hunt won the race and Niki was third.

Everything, in Championship terms, hung on the extra race tacked on for the season's end in Japan. There torrential rain made the circuit near impossible. Lauda's burned eyelids were troubling him badly every time he blinked and attempted to re-focus his eyes, and in such conditions he simply gave up. 'It's too dangerous to continue', he said, not blaming some mysterious 'feeling' in the car, but announcing his own cold decision. Was it cowardly, or was it courageous, are questions which will be asked as long as motor racing is discussed. For Niki Lauda it was the right decision, and he lives to fight another day. He had done more than enough to become the true hero of 1976 — whatever the superficial thinking of the mediamen might make of it. Niki Lauda himself, Ferrari World Champion, Viennese gentleman, could not give a damn what anybody else made of it all.

James Simon Wallis Hunt

BORN AUGUST 29, 1947, BELMONT, SURREY, ENGLAND

In winning a controversial World Championship title in 1976, James Hunt became the sixth Briton, and the fourth Englishman, ever to do so. His Championship season was undoubtedly the most sensational, most discussed and most highly publicised of all time for it included his finishing first in no less than seven World Championship-qualifying GP races to equal Jimmy Clark's 1963 record (although there were more races to win in 1976) and then being disqualified from two of them. Just to cap it all one of his docked victories was subsequently restored and in another qualifying round some highly dubious regulation juggling combined to give Hunt an enormous startline handicap and apparently wrecked his title chances. His late-season run of success to overcome this handicap, and to steal the World title by one point from an heroic Niki Lauda made Hunt a national hero to a general public fascinated by his well-promoted and highly promotable character and career.

Few would deny Hunt's incredible resilience, for throughout his formative racing years he showed a remarkable ability to bounce back from blows and disappointments which would have set a lesser man on the road to a quiet life outside the sport. There was a terrible time when James 'Shunt' was a bar-room joke. Then Lord Hesketh's youthful team put him into Formula 1 and with the right tools Hunt proved he could do a remarkably competitive job. When Hesketh's team collapsed Hunt was already a British public figure. When Hunt's wife left him for actor Richard Burton gossip columnists had a field day which served to promote the good-looking Hunt and his glamorous profession to superstar status. His extrovert and extremely articulate character was perfectly suited to inherit the Jackie Stewart public mantle of 'Mr Motor Racing' and when he took over Emerson Fittipaldi's place with the McLaren team for 1976 he was set for

Champion in focus – James Hunt and fan, 1976

the season which confirmed his 'Super Stardom'. To the *cognoscenti* perhaps he was not the outstanding driver of the year, and perhaps he simply showed well in a far from outstanding Grand Prix field. Some were alienated by his often arrogant and childish behaviour. Others were convinced that the sun beamed forth from his overalls leg and that this promotable British asset was genuinely the greatest racing driver the World had yet seen. The tall blond Briton was himself refreshingly objective about his own abilities, not regarding himself as another Fangio or Clark but happy with his ability to win and that – after all – was all that mattered.

James Hunt was born the son of a stockbroker and developed early sporting ability which took him to Junior Wimbledon as a tennis player and gave him County-class status at Squash. He saw his first motor race at eighteen and

was immediately hooked. He shared the kind of steely-eyed determination to make good which had brought forward Graham Hill from slightly more humble circumstances. Not that James Hunt was a moneyed young man. He had to work for his racing, and it started in 1967 with a mildly-tuned Mini. It was the best he could afford. He contested a handful of club races before the money ran out, but in 1968 part-talked part-drove himself into a sponsored Formula Ford drive in a Russell Alexis owned by Gowrings of Reading, a large Ford dealership. He had a good year, his name and that of his sponsor were regularly in the magazines, and Hunt was on his way.

Staying in Formula Ford for 1969 he did a deal with an outfit named Motor Racing Enterprises who teamed him with Dave Morgan in a pair of quasi-works Formula Ford Merlyns. The team does not appear to have been a happy one, and although Hunt did well early in the year, Morgan left; he carried on independently and in August of that year sank his money in an ancient Formula 3 Brabham BT21.

At Cadwell Park he leapt to prominence, finishing third in his heat and fourth in the final against Tim Schenken, Ronnie Peterson and another man putting up his first really good showing, Howden Ganley, who was later to become a BRM works

'James Shunt' in his Formula 3 days, running round outside the pack at Brands Hatch, 1971

driver. The prototype F3 March made its debut in this meeting, and after another fourth place in the old Brabham at Mallory Park, Hunt drove the car in Peterson's place at Brands Hatch in October, but could do no better than tenth. However, his performances during the year, in which he showed natural skill combined with that immense determination, earned him the second Grovewood Award as one of the year's most promising British drivers.

With this award as a springboard the 22-year old Hunt had his first full Formula 3 season in 1970 with a Molyslip-backed works Lotus 59. His ebullient driving became more polished after an early-season spate of incidents. In mid-season he won the important Rouen F3 race on the demanding Les Essarts circuit, but a September win at Zolder in Belgium was his only other first place of the year. He was second at Osterreichring, Oulton Park, Chimay, Knutsdorp and Brands Hatch in International events and was tipped for a Formula 2 ride in 1971.

That did not come until late in the year at Brands Hatch, where he showed well, while his Formula 3 season was desperately disappointing and marred by a string of stupid collisions and solo shunts which gained him his unwanted nickname. He suffered at the hands of less experienced drivers who were prepared to mix it in the underpowered hurly-burly of a new 1600cc Formula 3, yet when he did get clear of the pack he occasionally showed that he could leave them for dead in his Rose Bearings Marches. He won at Montlhéry, Nürburgring, Crystal Palace, and Brands Hatch but was overshadowed by the exploits of Roger Williamson and Dave Walker.

For 1972 March Engineering ran a works F3 team direct from their Bicester factory with STP sponsorship and Hunt was elected as team leader with Irishman Brendan McInerney buying the number two place. Failure was total, and after a fiery exchange at Monaco both drivers left the team. The youthful Lord Alexander Fermor-Hesketh was campaigning a Dastle F3 car at the time, and his motor racing advisor 'Bubbles' Horsley snapped up the redundant Hunt's services. The rest of the year saw a flurry of accidents and disappointments before the Dastle project was wound up, but the Hesketh was campaigning a Dastle F3 happy one — and was to flourish.

A road accident in which Hunt hurt himself punctuated what should have been a hopeless year, but Hesketh hired a year-old F2 March for him late in the season and James used it to considerable effect. In the final John Player Championship round at Oulton Park he led the works Marches of Ronnie Peterson and Niki Lauda before dropping back with a loose rear wing, and he was then fifth at Albi and fourth at Hockenheim to recoup something of his waining prestige.

The following season — 1973 — was to be the year in which Hunt finally made the grade, and in a sensational manner. After the Hesketh team's F2 Surtees had been destroyed in a Goodwood testing accident, his Lordship rented a Surtees F1 car for Hunt to drive in the early-season Brands Hatch Race of Champions. He drove intelligently to finish third in a race notable for retirements, behind Hulme's McLaren and Gethin's winning Formula 5000 Chevron-Chevrolet. Hesketh ordered a brand-new Formula 1 March 731 for his driver, and Horsley acquired the services of Dr Harvey Postlethwaite, the March development engineer, to go with it.

Hunt, Horsley and Postlethwaite rapidly welded themselves into a very effective team, and the ever-developing March — free of commercial sponsorship — became the sensation of the season. James ran sixth at Monaco before hitting trouble, missed the Swedish race to do some development testing, then returned sixth place and his maiden Championship point in the French GP and the Paul Ricard circuit, fourth and fastest lap in the British GP, third in Holland and ended the season with a sensationally close-fought second place right on Ronnie Peterson's tail in the United States GP at Watkins Glen.

In mid-season Hunt won the minor Avon Motor Tour of Britain in a Chevy Camaro saloon, and he was also to drive in CanAm for Shadow, in the Kyalami 1000Km race in a Gulf-Mirage sports car, in a Formula 5000 Eagle, in European Touring Car Championship BMWs and in the televised celebrity IROC touring car series in the USA.

With the death of Roger Williamson at Zandvoort, Hunt was alone as a British F1 newcomer, and when Tony Brise died in the Hill team air crash late in 1975 James became the sole English Formula 1 driver with all that considerable tradition to uphold.

During 1974 the Hesketh team should have been knocking on the door of success. They aimed first to win a non-Championship race, and then a Grand Prix. Which event was immaterial. Hunt won the non-Championship International Trophy Meeting at Silverstone but three thirds and a fourth were the best he could salvage from a Championship season dogged by unreliability and misfortune.

Come 1975 and Lord Hesketh was pulling in his motor racing horns. The trappings of a spare-no-expense travelling circus were sold off, camp followers jettisoned and under Horsley's capable management the team lived a hand-to-mouth existence

to survive from race to race. Old chassis were sold, prize money became all-important and Hunt rose to the occasion to finish a strong second after leading in Buenos Aires, won at Zandvoort after a well-timed tyre change, was second in France and Austria, fourth in Britain and the USA and fifth with a brand-new Hesketh 308C in Italy. He was fourth in the Drivers' Championship, and then came the blow as Hesketh pulled out and folded his team. Almost simultaneously Emerson Fittipaldi made his shock decision to abandon his McLaren seat for his brother Wilson's Copersucar set-up and Hunt rapidly stepped sideways into the Colnbrook drive.

Sponsored by Marlboro and Texaco, for whom he proved a vast asset in commercial promotions, Hunt began the incredible season which saw him start on pole position for the first race in Brazil only to crash mildly in the race. In South Africa Hunt was again on pole but was beaten into second

place by Lauda's Ferrari. At Long Beach Depailler shouldered him into a barrier and Hunt disgraced himself in the eyes of some people with what appeared to be a childish display of petulance which left his drivable McLaren abandoned by the roadside. In Spain Lauda was handicapped by damaged ribs, Hunt won, and the McLaren was found to be over the maximum legal width. He was disqualified, but after an appeal and many weeks of litigation, was reinstated. At Zolder Hunt's gearbox failed, and at Monaco his engine. In Sweden he was fifth on a circuit where McLaren cars have seldom worked. It looked as though his bolt was shot, but then came France where Hunt started from pole, won again – and heard that the Spanish victory had been restored to him.

The incredible British GP saw Hunt win fair and square in the restarted race in which he should not have been allowed to run, and again he was

subsequently disqualified from the results — and this time stayed disqualified despite more appeals and a public outcry. By this time the man in the black helmet had become anathema to the Italian racing press and public for his apparently dubious successes at Ferrari's expense. When Lauda crashed and was burned at the Nürburgring and Hunt won from pole position feeling in Italy ran high. When he muffed his chance in Austria, starting from his fifth pole position of the season, and came home fourth he seemed to be closing too slowly on Lauda's vast Championship lead. In Italy charges of illegal fuel came to a head when the McLarens were relegated to back-of-the-grid starting positions. In trying to stage a fight back Hunt optimistically expected Tom Pryce — the Welsh Shadow driver — to give him room into one of the tight chicanes, and as the McLaren bogged-down in loose aggregate to leave the race so another display of immaturity saw the English ace angrily pushing away marshals who were on the scene. The

Milanese crowd's 'evil eye' signs certainly paid off that black day.

It was after this tawdry episode that Hunt lost his British GP points, and in Canada and the USA he responded nobly 'to show two fingers to the lot of 'em' and his reliable McLaren operated perfectly to record two excellent wins. Into the final round at Japan's Mount Fuji circuit Hunt had to finish higher than fourth to steal the Championship from Lauda if the Austrian failed to score. When Niki pulled out of the race early the title looked assured for Hunt's leading McLaren, and after a dramatic late-race tyre change he finished third and stole the World Championship by one solitary point.

It was the conclusion of a season which would have done credit to a Hollywood script writer's imagination, and Hunt ended the year loaded with accolades and awards and looking forward to defending his World title in 1977 and perhaps proving himself finally as one of history's great rather than just good racing drivers.

That memorable weekend for McLaren's 1976 number one as he won the French GP at Ricard-Castellet and heard that his Spanish GP disqualification had been quashed at appeal. It was the start of the Championship charge which toppled Lauda, but not Ferrari

The Driver-Constructors

Jack Brabham was the man who caused all the trouble. When he proved that he could not only drive cars successfully but could also build them profitably, the idea caught on. It first rubbed off on Bruce McLaren — his one-time team-mate with Cooper — and then his own works driver, Dan Gurney, caught the bug. In later years John Surtees trod the rocky path, with less success, but McLaren and Gurney proved so good at their newfound craft that they deserve a chapter to themselves. . .

Bruce Leslie McLaren

Portrait of a nice guy — Bruce Leslie McLaren

Bruce was a New Zealander, an amiable, honest, clear-minded character whose great personal charm and natural modesty made him the most popular driver of his time. He was good in Grand Prix cars, an ace in sports cars, and a gifted practical engineer whose products perpetuated his name long after his tragic death . . . which most people who knew him still cannot really accept.

Bruce Leslie McLaren was born in Auckland, New Zealand, on August 30, 1937. His father, Leslie, ran a garage business in the smart suburb of Remuera, and with Bruce's three uncles had dominated local motorcycle sport for years.

At school Bruce was bright academically and a budding rugby footballer until at the age of nine the pains began in his left hip. It was the first sign of Perthe's Disease, a seizing of the joint, which put the McLarens' only son into a crippled children's home for 3 years.

Good treatment and the will to get better put Bruce back on his feet, but sports seemed history to him as he returned to school. Then he discovered rowing, and that helped him develop the broad shoulders so typical of him in later years. Only legacy of his illness was a pronounced limp, with his left leg an inch and a half shorter than the right, and as he crammed to catch up on his education, Pop McLaren had bought a 1929 Ulster Austin Seven for

racing. When the car was finally revived it proved diabolical, and Pop gave it to his son to gain practical engineering experience.

At 15 Bruce was driving the Ulster, and he took it into his first hill-climb competition at Muriwai, won his class and beat somebody called Phil Kerr in the process.

The two both had Austins and thereafter they prepared them together in the McLaren garage, and Pop shared drives with his son in the family Ulster. Late in 1954 he bought an Austin Healey 100, and when Bruce invested in an unsatisfactory Ford Special the following year, Pop cheered him up by letting him race the Healey.

Bruce was working on an engineering degree at Auckland University when the 1956 New Zealand Grand Prix was held on the nearby Ardmore Airfield, and there he raced the Healey in a supporting event, facing a visitor named Stirling Moss in a Porsche.

He was sufficiently successful with the Healey to think of better things, and the family bought Brabham's 1½-litre centre-seat Manxtail Cooper for 1957. Bruce corresponded with Brabham in England, and as the 1958 New Zealand season approached the Aus-tralian ace suggested that he should bring out two single-seater Coopers, and Bruce should drive one of them.

His prowess with that car and the Healey which had gone before won him the New Zealand International Grand Prix Association's 'Driver to Europe' Scholarship. He arrived in England in March, prepared his own car in Cooper's workshops and raced a season in 1½-litre Formula 2.

Proudest performance of that year was a win in the F2 section of the German Grand Prix. It was the eve of his twenty-first birthday, and a tremendous press greeted the precocious new talent from New Zealand.

For 1959 Charles and John Cooper took Bruce into their works team as number two to Jack Brabham, and he won that dramatic Grand Prix in Florida, was pipped on the line for second place in the British Grand Prix (by Moss) and was sixth in the World Championship.

The 1960 season started almost immediately, and Bruce won the opening round of the new Championship in Argentina, and trailed Brabham throughout the year to finish second to him in the World title.

Not until 1962 did he win again in

Luck was on McLaren's side this day in 1968 when he unwittingly won the Belgian Grand Prix at Spa after Stewart's leading Matra had run low on fuel. Here early in the race he locks a wheel in his own McLaren M7A on the entry to the tight La Source hairpin. Behind him are Rodriguez (BRM), Ickx (Ferrari) and Beltoise (Matra V12)

Formula 1 taking Cooper's last honours of the 1½-litre Formula, at Monaco and in the non-Championship race at Reims. Then Cooper's decline steepened, and although their cars were still strong and reliable, Bruce's smooth driving efforts could not make them race winners. He had become team leader on Brabham's departure, and he cleaned-up the Tasman races back home and had an early taste of American professional sports car racing on the West Coast.

For the 1964 Tasman Championship he wanted to field new Coopers, but the management were not keen and McLaren's muted frustration with their lack of development pumped life into Bruce McLaren Motor Racing Ltd. He went into partnership with his intended Tasman team-mate Timmy Mayer's brother Teddy — and they built 2·5-litre 'Cooper'-Climax cars in which Bruce again won the Tasman title. Poor Timmy Mayer died in an accident at Longford, Tasmania, but Teddy decided to stay with Bruce, and the team survived.

During 1964, they bought Roger Penske's controversial Zerex sports car and raced it briefly and successfully with its 2·7-litre Climax engine. In mid-season, with Bruce still strug-

gling along in Formula 1 with the increasingly uncompetitive Coopers, the Zerex was chopped about to accept a 3·5 litre Oldsmobile V8 and Bruce won with it first time out at Mosport in Canada. The McLaren name in big sports car racing was about to be made. . .

During the following season the small team signed a manufacturing agreement with Elva for their big-banger sports cars and Bruce was fiercely competitive in his. At the end of the year he left Cooper to concentrate on building and racing his own cars, and from that time the team looked back just once, and that was when they lost their founder.

For the first season of 3-litre Formula 1 racing Bruce's close-knit, happy team wrestled with a linered-down Indy Ford engine and a strong but hefty chassis, while in sports car racing he· and his team-mate Chris Amon lost the inaugural CanAm title to John Surtees and the Lolas.

Bruce had become a valued and vital member of the Ford GT team, and he and Amon shared Detroit's first victory in the Le Mans 24-Hours. Big cars were his speciality, and Bruce made no mistake in the CanAm Championship, which helped finance Cosworth-Ford

Bruce McLaren really shone when he drove his own big-engined CanAm sports cars. Here at Laguna Seca in 1969 he is sandwiched by Kiwi team-mates Chris Amon and Denny Hulme

engined Formula 1 McLarens for 1968. Bruce won first time out with the new cars, in the Race of Champions at Brands Hatch, and team-mate Denny Hulme came within an ace of winning the World title. At Spa Bruce was a surprised winner of the Belgian Grand Prix, and into 1969 he went on winning in CanAm cars and proving a consistent front runner, though not a winner, in Grands Prix.

The McLaren team was acknowledged to be the best-organised outfit in the business. Bruce's bright personality proved a major attraction for big-money sponsors, and the efficient Teddy Mayer and that same Phil Kerr against whom Bruce had raced in his first hill-climb, provided clockwork management administration.

Several times Bruce felt he should give up driving to concentrate upon the pure engineering side of his blossoming business, but there was never a suitable driver available to take his place. In any case he would have continued test-driving, for deep and exhaustive testing were vital ingredients in the team's huge CanAm success, and their competitive showings in Formula 1.

It was, perhaps, tragically fitting that the stocky, personable Kiwi's luck should run out in a testing accident rather than in some minute misjudgement in the heat of a race. It did just that shortly after 12.22 pm on the afternoon of Monday, June 1, 1970.

Bruce had been testing the prototype McLaren M8D on the team's familiar experimental venue at Goodwood, sheltering beneath the Sussex Downs. As he nosed the big car into a gentle kink in the main straight at near maximum speed, its engine cover lifted, caught the slipstream and slammed open. In that instant the rear wheels were snatched off the road, and the bright papaya-coloured car raced off course and slammed into a marshal's point which had to be standing in McLaren's wayward path. The CanAm King, one of motor racing's genuinely nice guys, died instantly. . .

Daniel Sexton 'Dan' Gurney

Dan Gurney — America's best road racer of the 1960s, a man who perhaps fumbled himself out of massive success, creator of the Eagle racing car marque

In 1967, the year before Bruce McLaren had scored that fortuitous win in the Belgian Grand Prix, Spa's top honour had fallen to Dan Gurney and his Eagle. The tall, boyish Californian thus became the first American in a more-or-less American car to win a *Grande Epreuve* since Murphy's Duesenberg in 1921. It was to be his only Grand Prix victory in his own car, but the Gurney-Eagles later made a terrific impact upon the American racing scene.

Daniel Sexton Gurney was born on April 13, 1931, in Port Jefferson, Long Island, NY. His father, John Gurney, was a talented operatic singer, who spent nine years with the Metropolitan. The family moved around America, following the shows, and in 1937 and 1938 Dan had his first sight of motor racing, when he was taken to see the Vanderbilt Cup at Roosevelt Raceway, Long Island.

He was immediately hooked, and at

In his days as a works driver Gurney is chopped-off at Rouen's Nouveau Monde hairpin by driver-constructor Jack Brabham, Lotus mounted for the 1962 French GP. Dan won a race of attrition, joined Brabham's team for 1963–65, then became a constructor in his own right

13 was tagging around with a bunch of older boys who haunted Freeport Stadium's midget racing. In 1948 he bought his first car, a 1933 Ford roadster, and when John Gurney moved his family to California, they settled in Riverside, outside Los Angeles and a hot-bed of the West Coast hot-rod movement.

Academic studies took second place to a growing involvement in hot-rodding, and in 1950 'Daniel S. Gurney' clocked 130 mph on Bonneville salt flats in a Mercury Special which he had prepared himself. It was his first major competitive outing.

As the Korean War raged, Gurney joined the US Army and served in an anti-aircraft unit for the last four months of the conflict, but saw no action. He took up table tennis, and became unofficial champion of the Inchon NCO Club!

The game served to sharpen his reflexes, and back in civilian life late in 1954 he took a job with a Riverside engineering company He saved enough cash to buy a Triumph TR2, and placed third in class in his first road race, at Torrey Pines, in October 1955. From the TR2 he graduated to a Porsche Spyder, and his fast driving,

tempering fire with cool car control, attracted drives for many private entrants.

In 1957 Frank Arciero offered him a drive in his 4·9-litre Ferrari, and Dan made the most of the opportunity by winning three of his first six races in it. Phil Hill was suitably impressed by the lanky (6 ft 2 in) 26-year-old, and recommended him to Luigi Chinetti. He invited Dan to Sebring in 1958, although the drive did not materialise, but then came his European debut in a Ferrari at Le Mans. He followed up with a drive into seventh place at the Nürburgring in a sports OSCA, and he led the Reims 12-Hours in a Ferrari before co-driver André Guelfi crashed it.

Romolo Tavoni, the Ferrari team manager, had been tipped by Chinetti to watch the promising Californian, and when Mike Hawthorn informed Ferrari of his retirement, Gurney was flown to Italy for serious test drives. Tavoni signed him on immediately, and Gurney's promise was such that he found himself in a Formula 1 works car before the end of the 1959 season.

He made his debut in the French Grand Prix at Reims, where he ran sixth, and when Jean Behra stormed out of the team — tragically to lose his life in a Porsche sports car within weeks — Gurney was equipped with good machinery. He rose to the occasion, placed second in Germany, third in Portugal and fourth in Italy to take seventh place in his first World Championship competition — after just a half-season's racing.

Ferrari had given him a good start, but the independent and quietly-spoken Californian disliked their binding contracts, and signed for BRM in the new year. It was to be an unhappy season with their difficult new rear-engined cars, and at Zandvoort he ploughed off the track when a brake

ship standings, having been second in three Grands Prix. In the following season he caustically likened the new flat-eight Porsche's power and handling to a VW Beetle, but it was reliable and other peoples' troubles gave him his first Grand Prix victory — in the French race at Rouen.

He drove in all manner of American races, including Indianapolis in one of Mickey Thompson's cars, and he took a guest along with him to the Speedway. It was Colin Chapman, whose Lotus 25 monocoque car was on its way, and Gurney felt sure that such a car, bred in Grand Prix racing, fitted

hose fractured and the car killed an 18-year-old boy spectating in a prohibited area. Dan injured an arm and his ribs, and suffered agonies from the boy's death.

For long weeks he thought of giving up the sport which had ensnared him, but such thoughts rapidly faded as he drove in more and more events after the accident. He won his last race for BRM, at Ballarat in Australia, early in 1961, and then signed for Porsche as their Formula 1 team leader.

The flat-four air-cooled German cars were fast enough and reliable, and Dan ended a good season equal third with Stirling Moss in the World Champion-

with an American Ford V8 engine, could win at Indy.

So the Lotus-powered-by-Ford marriage came about, and in 1963–64 Dan drove for Chapman's team at Indy, and in 1965 drove a private Lotus-Ford of his own. Jimmy Clark won the race for Lotus and Ford of Detroit in that latter season, but Gurney — whose idea the whole thing had been — never bettered his original seventh place in the Lotus-Ford of 1963.

That season had seen Dan moving to the Brabham Racing Organisation for Formula 1, and there he proved himself one of the top four drivers,

Gurney wrought the Chapman Lotus/Ford engine partnership which finally won Indy for Jimmy Clark in 1965. Here he poses on the pit apron with his Lotus-Ford crew before the 1963 race. In later years his own Eagles placed second in the '500', while others would win it

each of whom was fully capable of winning a Grand Prix. He led and lost, time after time, and while Jack Brabham moved quietly into the background, Dan spearheaded the green-and-gold car team. In 1964 at Rouen his luck and his car held together and he won his second French Grand Prix — fair and square. In Mexico he won again, when Jimmy Clark's car and his Championship hopes failed on the very last lap, and Dan's victory gave the World title to John Surtees, second in the race.

What had become known as 'Gurney Luck' persisted through 1965 and kept him out of good results, but any sportsman can largely make his own luck and Dan had won himself a reputation as a 'meddler', always juggling with his car's settings at the last moment and usually introducing some problem which foiled him time after time.

As the introduction of the 3-litre Formula drew near for 1966, Gurney announced that he would be leaving Brabham to set up his own racing car manufacturing business and racing team. He went into partnership with Carroll Shelby — the Californian racing driver turned Cobra constructor — and with backing from Goodyear, Mobil, Bardahl and other companies the AAR empire was formed. There were two divisions; All-American Racers based at Santa Ana in California who were to build Indianapolis cars, and Anglo-American Racers based at Rye in Sussex who were to produce Formula 1 cars powered by Weslake-designed V12 engines. Always intensely patriotic, Dan Gurney was realising a long-cherished dream of producing an American Grand Prix car. He chose Eagle — America's national emblem — as the name for his cars, and hired Len Terry — whose Lotus 38 had just won Indy — to design them.

In Formula 1 the Gurney-Eagles suffered similar unreliability to Dan's Brabhams of the 1½ litre years, and the Weslake engines proved supremely powerful but manufacturing problems were never adequately resolved. Dan's victory at Spa came on a rare occasion when everything 'clicked' and went on clicking for a full race distance, but into 1968 his backers began to realise that Grand Prix racing offered little return, and after he retired with no oil pressure from the Italian Grand Prix Anglo-American Racers was run-down, and closed.

Gurney hired a McLaren for the late-season races — Bruce having driven briefly for the team in 1967 after Richie Ginther had retired from racing — and was not to reappear in Formula 1 until after Bruce's death in 1970, when he drove works McLarens briefly in Grand Prix and CanAm races until sponsorship clashes forced him to abandon the idea.

Thus the likable Californian's Grand Prix career simply fizzled out, but meanwhile the now Tony Southgate-designed Indianapolis and Formula A Eagles had been produced in great numbers, and had proved very successful. At Indy, Dan drove a 5-litre stock-block engined version to second place in 1968 and 1969, and in a new car he was third in 1970. Bobby Unser won the '500' for Eagle in 1968, and the Formula A Championship also came Santa Ana's way.

Dan Gurney was a man who could drive any kind of car supremely competitively. He excelled in Formula 1, long-distance sports cars, CanAm sports cars, stock cars — winning the Riverside road race in three consecutive years — and in Indianapolis-type events. His happiest time in road racing must have been June, 1967, when he won the Belgium GP in his own car, and shared first place at Le Mans with A. J. Foyt — driving a Ford Mark IV. After he retired from race driving at the end of 1970, his black helmeted figure, looming out of the cockpit of his cars, was sadly missed, but Eagle went from strength to strength, with cars designed by Roman Slobodinskij proving themselves oval-track pace-setters and dominating USAC racing to a considerable degree. Dan Gurney gained a great deal from motor racing, but on balance he is one of the rare great drivers who has put back much more than he took out. He and Bruce McLaren are two of a kind . . . and there aren't enough of those.

Men from a Different World

American motor racing diverged from European development in its earliest years. Since the Second World War the two have slowly grown together, but the current great names of American motor sport are still a different breed. Although some excel equally on road and track, their's is a World apart.

While a top Grand Prix driver might get by on as few as eleven races a year, one of the American aces would probably be doing sixty-plus, building his sport into a virtual industry and earning his money with sheer blood, sweat, toil and perhaps the occasional tear.

A. J. Foyt

No man has worked harder at his racing business than the iron man of American motor sport; Anthony Joseph Foyt Jr, known invariably as 'A.J.' A Texan, from Houston, Foyt was born on January 16, 1936. He started racing in his home town as early as 1953, joined USAC four years later and drove his first Indy 500 in one of the unresponsive front-engined roadsters in 1958. From that point on he never looked back. Today he has amassed more Championship points than any other driver in history; he is the only man ever to have won five National Championship titles; he has covered more racing miles at Indianapolis than any other man; he is the only active four-time '500' winner; the only driver to have started the last 20 500s, and he has led Indianapolis for more laps than any other man. Add to this the All-American Le Mans 24-Hours win which he achieved with Dan Gurney in a 7-litre Ford in 1967, and you have an idea of the man's sheer sporting achievement.

A. J. Foyt's first National Championship was clinched in 1960, when his bullish strength and stamina pulled off wins in four of the last five 100-mile dirt races to compensate for retirement in the prestigious '500'. The following year saw him retain his Championship and win Indy for the first time, and in 1964 he took enormous delight in beating the rear-engined 'funny cars' in his big roadster to score the last Indy victory for a front-engined car. When his own distantly Lotus-based Coyote won the '500' in 1967, the gruff, tough Texan's winnings for those three races alone totalled $443,52. His three other National Championships were taken in 1963–64 and 1967, and he was runner-up in 1962 and 1965. He took to racing USAC stock cars in the former runner-up season, and took the Stock Championship in 1968 for Ford. He dabbled with big sports cars in the mid-1960s, and has also won NASCAR stock events on the speedways at Daytona, Atlanta and Ontario.

In many ways Foyt has been America's Jack Brabham; just as effective a driver while no artist behind the wheel; just as much a non-communicator; and just as clever! Behind his monosyllabic facade, more bearish than Denny Hulme in his blackest mood, Foyt has proved himself an extremely astute operator, and a master of 'psyching' the opposition with both words and deeds.

In 1966 the parallel between the jut-chinned Texan and the dark-chinned Australian was extended, when the first Coyote cars were built, in Long Beach, California, for that year's '500'. Unfortunately A.J. crashed the prototype on the first day of qualification, and for 1967 A. J. Foyt Jr Enterprises Inc was established at Houston to build the new Coyotes which won at Indy.

Foyt was working closely with his USAC Championship as his originally Ford-built Foyt V8 turbocharged engines became the things to beat. At Ontario and Indianapolis nobody qualified within two mph of the Coyote. A.J. won the California 500 after leading all the way, and looked set to win the 500 for a record-breaking fourth time when his Coyote was damaged by debris from a crashed competitor. He ended the year as National Champion once more, and in

'AyJay' Foyt – upholding the establishment at Indianapolis in 1964 when the European road-race bred rear-engined cars failed and allowed him to score the final victory for the traditional Offy-engined roadster

father, A.J. Sr, and in 1969 they acquired Ford's existing stockpile of quad-cam V8 engines and parts. From that point on the famous V8, now in turbocharged form, carried Foyt's name cast proudly on the cam covers, and other customers had to come to him for their motive power. Unfortunately for Foyt, the turbo Offy engines were proving more effective by this time, and his fortunes took a dive until 1974 when his V8 engine responded better to restricted tuning regulations and he returned to the winner's circle.

Foyt at forty dominated the 1975

1976 the irascible Texan was again frustrated in his bid to become Indy's first four-time winner. He was second to Johnny Rutherford's McLaren when the race was stopped after only 255 miles due to rain. Despite the V8 engine approaching its development limit, A.J. qualified on pole for more than half the Championship Trail races, won two of them and usually led the others from the start, but the Championship crown slid from his grasp. Still this perennial performer goes on, an ageless grizzled veteran in the grizzliest mould of all.

Mario Andretti

The closest man to Foyt in USAC standings is Mario Andretti, a diminutive little man from Nazareth, Pennsylvania, who came to America at 17 as an immigrant from Italy.

He made his name in a little under four minutes at Indy in 1965. In fact it took him just 3-minutes 46·63-seconds to put his Brawner-Ford on a brief pole position for the Indianapolis 500. It was his first drive at the Speedway, and in the race he was just pipped into third place. During that month of May the promising young

Champions frame 'SuperWop' – Stewart and Hulme with the World's greatest all-rounder, Mario Gabriele Andretti

Driving for Ferrari meant a lot to the Italian-born American. Here he drives the fearsome Ferrari 712 in a CanAm race at Watkins Glen, 1971

kid from the dirt tracks became 'Rookie of the Year' and a star overnight. By the end of the season he was National Champion, and the following season he was Champion again. In 1967 and 1968 he was runner-up for the title and in 1969 he won it for the third time. Then came a Grand Prix debut for the Lotus team, a much-dreamed of place with Ferrari, and a win in the South African Grand Prix in 1971. At that point Andretti's cup was nearly full. The World Championship was his ultimate ambition, but USAC commitments chopped too much from his Formula 1 programme, and not until 1975 did he manage a full season.

Andretti was the little man who could race and win in any kind of car.

He won on dirt and paved ovals, in stock cars on the high-banked superspeedways, in Championship cars on road and track circuits, in long-distance sports car classics, in Formula 1 and in Formula 5000. Seldom had there been a more versatile, or more deeply competitive all-round driver, and perhaps if his background had been a little different we could be comparing him with Fangio, or Clark or Stewart as one of the greatest of all time. As it is he falls a little short of such judgement. . .

Mario Gabriele Andretti and his brother Aldo were born as twins on February 28, 1940, on a farm just outside Trieste in the borderland between Italy and Yugoslavia. Papa

Andretti was a farmer, but at the end of the war his land was swallowed as the frontier was adjusted. The family wanted to remain Italian and they joined hordes of refugees shuffling westwards.

They were settled in a refugee camp at Lucca in 1948, and lived there for seven years — one of 27 families in one large hut. It was in Lucca that the teenage twins began hanging around a

twin had fallen off the top of a truck while *watching* the racing.

Sadly Aldo was never again to be as accomplished as his brother, and after sustaining severe head injuries in a sprint car crash in 1969 he never drove again — and became manager of his brother's Firestone tyre stores.

From 1958–1960 Mario won over 20 modified stock car races and in 1961 moved into Sprint car racing in

The Vel's Parnelli Formula 1 effort failed when its promoters realised that just a lot of money does not win in Grand Prix racing. Andretti always drove his hardest, and seldom harder than here in the 1975 British GP after a dislodged nose canard upset the car's handling

local garage, and they had their first racing experience in a little Stanguellini which the garagist had bought for his son.

Then the family emigrated to Nazareth where relations already resided, and three days after their arrival Mario and Aldo heard the rumble of stock cars racing on a local track and were instantly hooked.

Their uncle, Louis Messenlehner, helped teach them the language and — clandestinely — to build a Hudson stocker of their own. They began racing it in 1958, just barely 17 and swearing blind they were 21, and Aldo won first time out. Aldo crashed and suffered a bad concussion, and Mario had a bad time convincing his parents that his

the rough-and-tumble world unknown to Europeans. In the 1963 season he drove 107 races in what he describes as 'the most constructive racing I ever did' and it was there that he learned all the arts of crowded race driving and the skilled control of a high-powered car on dirt.

He joined USAC in 1964 but was lost with the front-engined roadsters on paved ovals. He was used to hurling Sprint cars about on dirt and this was a completely new science. Slowly he clicked, and gained a plum drive with Al Dean's track team after regular driver Chuck Hulse injured himself.

It was with Dean and chief mechanic Clint Brawner that Mario made his name, and when Dean died in 1967 the

Right at the end of 1976 Andretti brought Lotus back to the winner's circle in the Japanese Grand Prix

broad-shouldered little Italian-born ace ran the team himself until major backing from Andy Granatelli's STP Corporation came along. He triumphed for them at Indianapolis in 1969, and in 1972 he moved to join Parnelli Jones and the Vel's Parnelli racing team.

He had Al Unser and Joe Leonard as USAC team mates in this outfit, and they enjoyed most success that season with the latter earning the National Championship on consistency. He drove in four GPs for Ferrari and was seventh at Monza on what seems to be his home ground in spirit if not by naturalisation. Mario also starred in the Ferrari sports car team, winning the Daytona Continental, Sebring 12-Hours and BOAC 1000 Km consecutively to open the Championship of Makes season, sharing these drives with Jacky Ickx. At the end of the year they added the Watkins Glen 6-Hours to their tally — Andretti had won all three US sports car classics.

In 1973 fortunes took a tumble although Mario set a closed circuit record at Texas Speedway of 214 mph! He was out of Formula 1 and out of luck with the latest Parnelli USAC cars. The next season saw Vel's Parnelli in Formula 1 in the closing races of the season. Mario placed seventh in Canada and qualified briefly on pole at Watkins Glen. Following

victory in the USAC Midget Championship and a good win for Alfa Romeo in the early-season Monza 1000 Km, *SuperWop* was clearly on his way back.

During 1975 the Team USA Formula 1 project never fulfilled its elegant promise although Mario scored with fourth in Sweden and fifth in France. He missed only the Belgian and Dutch GPs to fulfil USAC commitments, and the later absence saw him winning the Pocono 500. His F5000 Lola was pipped to the US Championship by English emigre Brian Redman's.

Early in 1976 Mario joined Team Lotus, and as the Type 77 was progressively developed he proved himself increasingly competitive. He capped what was virtually a come-back season by winning the Japanese GP by a clear lap after a remarkably intelligent drive, and embarked on a second Lotus season (despite some reservations about Formula 1-size retainers) with their new Type 78 'ground-effects car'.

Mario Andretti is primarily what he would call 'an ent'usiast', and his fast, spectacular yet heady style, articulate public skills, and Italian 'heart' has won him a vast (largely female) following.

Above all Mario is unmatched as the greatest all-rounder of his time, and possibly (since Moss never tackled track racing) of all time.

The Unser Family

The Unser dynasty was founded by Swiss immigrants who settled in Colorado just before the First World War. Nearby was the challenging dirt road to the summit of Pike's Peak, and in 1915 their sons, Jerry, Josef and Louis, were the first to reach the summit on motor cycles. When the Pike's Peak hill-climb became a spectacular national event, Joe placed second in it from 1926–29. He died while testing a car prior to the Indianapolis 500 — crashing on a road near Denver. Jerry was not such an accomplished driver but he made a name building hill-climb cars, and some family friction with Louis caused him to move to Albuquerque, New Mexico, where he brought up four sons; Louis Jr, Jerry Jr, Bobby and Al. They grew up imbued with motor sport, and while uncle Louis went on to become 'Old Man Mount'n', racing regularly at Pike's Peak, his nephews were hot on his tail.

Louis Jr twice won the Peak climb, but in 1964 he crashed heavily when unable to brake hard enough. . . He was losing his physical control, his sight was fading and doctors diagnosed multiple sclerosis. Thus the eldest son was forced out of a sport he loved, and concentrated his unimpaired intellectual abilities on running a successful speed shop business.

His twin brother, Jerry Jr, won the stock car division at the Peak around which so much of the family fortunes revolved, and was 1957 USAC Stock Champion. In 1958 he escaped from the gigantic multiple accident at Indianapolis which claimed Pat O'Connor's life, and then in practice there for the 1959 race he crashed heavily and suffered severe burns. He succumbed to pneumonia in hospital.

The younger brothers weathered these tragedies, and have today become two of the nation's greatest drivers. Bobby, born on February 20, 1934, had begun driving modified stock cars in New Mexico when still only 15. He won the state Championship in 1950–51, and then took to

The elder Unser — Bobby

Midget and Sprint single-seaters. In 1956 he won the Championship car class at the inevitable Peak, and from 1958 he won it consecutively six more times! In 1963 he made his Indy debut, but hit the wall on the third lap, and in 1964 was involved in the fiery first-lap disaster which killed Eddie Sachs and Dave MacDonald, and from which Jack Brabham escaped so fortuitously. Bobby went on battling around the Championship Trail, and 1967 was a great season which found him placing third in the National Championship with an Eagle. The following year was even better, and he won the Indianapolis 500 to delirious joy from his supporters, won Pike's Peak for the ninth time and took the Unser clan's first National Championship title by a narrow margin from Andretti.

He was enticed to BRM to drive in Grand Prix events, but his uncompromising driving of the fragile British car did not make for realistic racing, and a solitary outing in the United States Grand Prix convinced him of his station in life.

In 1970 Bobby began to be overshadowed by his more stylish brother Al, but late in the season he joined Dan Gurney's works Eagle team and in qualification for the 1972 '500' he shattered the racing world by qualifying at an average of 195·940mph. His

fastest lap was a new record at 196·678 mph and he led imperiously for the first 30 laps until the car's distributor rotor broke. He was fastest qualifier for eight of his nine Championship races that season, won four of them, and at Ontario became the first driver in USAC history to qualify for a race at over 200 mph — averaging 201·965 mph for his four laps!

The 1973 Indy race saw Bobby Unser qualifying second fastest at 198·183 mph and leading for the first 39 laps, but bad luck and continual mechanical failures robbed him of real success. A late season crash at Phoenix destroyed his mercurial Eagle and injured him, but he was soon back in harness, and racing on as hard as ever.

Meanwhile Al Unser had achieved remarkable stature as a USAC Championship Trail driver, perhaps not quite so brutally fast as his brother, but always competitive, smooth, thoughtful, calm and easy on his cars.

Five years Bobby's junior, Al was born on May 29, 1939, and he too cut his driving teeth on modifed stock cars, starting around Albuquerque in 1957, when he was 18. Naturally he went to try his skill on the daunting venue of Pike's Peak, and he was second there to Bobby in 1960 and 1962, and finally broke big brother's grasp on the event when he won it in 1964.

Al learned his car control and race-craft just like Bobby before him on the Sprint and Midget car circuits, and he made his Indianapolis debut in 1965, soldiering along with typical smooth reserve to finish ninth. The STP Corporation signed him as Jimmy Clark's Indy team-mate in a Lotus for 1966, but something appeared to break in the car for he spun into a wall after 161 of the 200 laps, while running third and ahead of eventual winner, Graham Hill.

He was luckier in the following year, when he finished second, and early in 1968 he tried his hand at NASCAR stock car racing at Daytona, placing fourth in their money-rich 500-mile classic, and was voted 'Rookie of the Year'. Back at Indy his luck ran out when a wheel came off his car and it smashed into the wall again at terrific speed. It was destroyed and Al was lucky to escape virtually unscathed. But he won five other races in a row, and ended the season third in the Championship behind Bobby.

In 1969 he was horsing around on a motor cycle at Indy and fell and broke a leg, which caused him to miss the '500' he so wanted to win. Then the first two Indianapolis 500s of the 1970s fell to his Vel's Parnelli Jones-entered Colt-Ford. In 1970 he started the race from pole and led for 190 of the 200 laps; he also won nine other Championship races, all five dirt events and was leading the California 500 by miles with only 14 laps to go when his car's turbocharger failed. His total of 5130 points was a new one-season record, and he won the National Championship to emulate his illustrious brother who was runner-up for the title. It was the first time brothers had achieved this unique result.

In 1971 Al Unser won Indy once more, and stole five of the season's first six races. It looked as though no-body could live with the younger Unser until mid-season, when his fortunes turned bad and he failed to score a single point in the remainder of the year, and lost his title.

Since that time Al Unser has been recognised as probably the smoothest and most intelligent driver on the USAC circuits, and he has continued winning for Vel's Parnelli although without the dominant form shown in those halcyon days of 1970.

Peter Revson

Gulf McLaren drivers at Indy in 1973 – Peter Revson (left) with pole man Johnny Rutherford. Revson the road racer shone brightly on the specialised USAC ovals

Two of America's greatest contemporary drivers were raised in Sports Car Club of America road events, and yet proved themselves equally at home on the oval speedways. They were the late Peter Revson and Mark Donohue, without mention of whom no work on great American racing drivers of our age would be complete.

While Foyt tops USAC's active driver list, Andretti is second with the Unser brothers hot on his tail, Bobby third and Al fourth. But there has been more to America's font of driving skill than these predominantly left-turn only racers. While Andretti's immigrant skills proved themselves immensely versatile, Peter Revson's glamorous image grew and grew in the 1970s to show winning form on road and track circuits, and the wealthy, handsome New Yorker came to typify the modern clean-cut American in International motor sport. As such he was a worthy successor to Phil Hill and Dan Gurney, but while they were essentially 'mechanics' he was a pure driver, and he had *style*.

Born on February 27, 1939, Peter Jeffrey Revson was an Easterner, son

of one of the founders of the Revlon cosmetics empire. Contrary to the popular impression, he was not heir to the Revlon fortunes, for his father left the organisation in 1958. Even so, he had something of a little rich boy upbringing, and he did not like it. He moved on to study mechanical engineering at Cornell, then did some brief 'general studies' at Columbia before winding up in Hawaii.

He had seen some SCCA sports car racing which fascinated him and while in Hawaii he celebrated his 21st birthday, took his Morgan street car to a meeting on Kahuku Point Airstrip, and drove it so wildly the stewards suggested he never return. His mother watched that first race, she never watched another, and 'Revvy' raced under a cloud of parental distaste thereafter.

Back on the mainland he worked a few frustrating months in the jungle of Madison Avenue's advertising agencies, then bought a flashy Italian Formula Junior which introduced him to the class in which he drove through 1961–62.

He felt that since FJ was the secondary Formula in Europe while just forming a club class in the United States, a transatlantic trip would be in order to gain some experience and perhaps a little recognition. So he arrived on the European scene in 1963, beat Timmy Mayer in a similar Cooper to win the Copenhagen GP at Roskilde,

Above: battered but unconcerned — 'Revvy' leaping his noseless Lotus 24 over one of the Nürburgring yumps during the 1964 German Grand Prix. Eight years later he won a works Formula 1 drive with McLaren, two years after that he was killed by a car failure in South Africa

1971 was Revson's arrival year as he won the CanAm Championship for McLaren, won pole position at Indianapolis and took second place for them in the '500' and won a Ken Tyrrell works team drive at Brands Hatch late in the season. His outing ended ignominiously in the bank at Paddock Hill, and like most drivers who bend Ken's cars, Revvy did not get a second try.

Then he did a deal with Tim Parnell to drive a BRM-engined spaceframe Lotus 24 in the Oulton Park Gold Cup race. It was his Formula 1 debut, with indifferent machinery and relatively limited experience; he finished ninth. One reporter wrote: 'The Formula Junior driver Revson was a bit untidy and tended to do Junior tricks, such as going into corners too fast on the wrong line when in company with more experienced drivers . . .'

The easily excited Revson took note of such criticism, and in 1964 he ran his own Lotus 24-BRM under the Parnell banner, carrying attractive Lola body panels and American colours of blue and white.

During that season Revvy picked up little more than experience and a few bob in start money. He did not catch on with any of the Formula 1 teams, but Ron Harris offered him Formula 3 and occasional Formula 2 drives in his semi-works Lotus team. He won the Monaco Formula 3 race in his best drive yet, but still nobody took note; the impression that he was a little rich boy playing at racing still abounded, although as he said: 'When I decided to go to Europe I was committing myself totally to professionalism and to a career in race driving. I wanted to go right to the top . . .'

In the American Fall series of sports car races, Revvy drove a 2-litre Brabham for Bill Kay, and won the class at Mosport, Kent, Laguna Seca and Riverside. He won more money than anyone else in the class, and for 1966 latched onto Skip Scott who had talked Essex Wire into running a long-distance sports car team with Ford GT40s. They contracted former Vanwall team manager David Yorke to run the operation, and David recalls the 26-year-old Revson as being '. . . very good, even then better than most people would have thought him. It was all there, but was he ever temperamental! The slightest thing and he

would go up like a balloon!'

In the Fords, Revson and Scott led their class at Daytona, Le Mans and the Nürburgring, and won it at Sebring and Monza to contribute more than any other team to Ford's victory in the Manufacturers' Championship.

By this time he had matured into a heady, steady driver who had speed on tap if it was needed. At the end of the season he put in some impressive drives in a CanAm McLaren, and for the next five seasons he stayed in America, building himself a career.

He raced successfully for Mercury, American Motors, and Shelby Mustang in Trans-Am, and drove Lola and McLaren cars in CanAm. In 1968 the monster 7-litre McLaren-Ford punched Peter Revson home to win the Fuji 'JapAm' race outside Tokyo, and in the following season fortune broke his way.

Goodyear arranged him an Indy ride in Jack Brabham's second car, and from 33rd and last place on the grid he soared through the 500-mile field to finish fifth. As a Speedway racer the Repco-Brabham was too slow, but as a road racer it was terrific, and a few weeks later Revson won at Indianapolis Raceway Park.

He was still regarded as a steady back-up driver rather than as an ace, but he did quite well with an ageing Lola in CanAm and went into 1970 to find an Indy ride with Gulf-McLaren in place of Chris Amon who could not come to terms with the Speedway. He ran seventh until a piston seized, while at Sebring he co-drove with actor Steve McQueen to steal a Porsche into second place. In CanAm he was McLaren's main opposition in a Lola entered by American distributor, Carl Haas. His performances there and in Roger Penske's TransAm Matador finally proved the latent talent which had been there for so many years.

In 1971, Peter Revson reached full stature, took pole position and placed second at Indy in his works McLaren, and then took to CanAm as Denny Hulme's team-mate, beat 'The Bear' and Jackie Stewart to win five rounds and became the first American CanAm Champion. His winnings for the season in McLaren cars grossed $306676, and at last Peter Revson had 'arrived'.

In the following season he found his way into McLaren's Formula 1 Grand Prix team, and put up a string of neat and smooth performances which yielded second place to Stewart and a start on pole position in Canada, and third places in South Africa, Britain and Austria. He drove for Alfa Romeo in a few sports car events and in the USAC McLarens qualified second quickest at Indianapolis, Ontario (for the California 500) and Pocono (for the Shaeffer 500) but hit trouble in every race.

During 1973 he served a second season in the Grand Prix arena, driving the Yardley-backed McLarens, and he was second in South Africa, beat a depleted field handsomely at Silverstone to score his first *Grande Epreuve* victory, and followed up with a controversial win in the rain at Canada's Mosport Park. He was the first American driver to win a *Grande Epreuve* since Dan Gurney in 1967 at Spa, and he finished fifth in the Championship table. His McLaren-Offy was on pole for the Ontario and Pocono 500s, but trouble sidelined it in both these important events, as it had at Indianapolis.

For the new year Revvy (like Rindt before him a well-heeled man to whom money was still all important) was given a valuable contract by Universal Oil Products and their Shadow team, and this should have been his year in an American-backed Grand Prix car. But it was not to be for on March 22, something failed in the Shadow's front-end while Peter was running fast at Kyalami. The car speared straight off the track, smashed through an Armco barrier and burst into flames. Graham Hill, Denny Hulme and Emerson Fittipaldi all stopped and leaped from their cars to help extricate him from the fire, but the good American driver with the playboy image he hated so much was already beyond help.

His death was sorely felt, in England and Europe as much as in his home country. The media made much of it, for it followed shortly after Cevert's fatal crash at Watkins Glen in a similar impact with an Armco barrier, and Revvy's name had been linked with Marjorie Wallace, at that time a recently unfrocked Miss World. This was the kind of attention the elegant Revson hated. His fuse was easily lit most of the time, although he could equally be very relaxed, entertaining and informative with people who were as enthusiastic about his sport as he was himself. The way the yellow press kept their mind below his belt needled him intensely. He had lived in a luxury apartment overlooking the Pacific at California's Redondo Beach, and in the

The first Formula 1 victory — Revvy's McLaren M23 on its way to victory against an accident decimated field in the 1973 British GP at Silverstone. Later in the year he won the rain-affected Canadian GP . . . it was his lucky season

Marina next door he kept a succession of power cruisers which were his great pride and joy. He was also in partnership with Peyton Cramer in a Lincoln-Mercury dealership, and early in 1972 when I was talking to him about racing safety he made his views plain. There had been tragedy in the family, four years previously, when his younger brother Douggie was killed in an F3 crash at Roskilde, where he himself had won his first race in Europe. He said; 'Motor racing is a sport like any other. There'll be winners, and there'll be losers; it's a game of skill, and if a man makes a mistake he shouldn't have to die for it. It'll show in the results, 'cos he'll lose time, just like if a sprinter trips, or a baseball player strikes out.

'I always drive as though if I leave the road I'm going to do myself some damage, but really it would make no difference if there was a rubber cushion waiting to soften the blow. There's always the inbuilt time penalty, and even putting a wheel on the dirt slows you down. But I think time's all you should stand to lose — not your life. The name of the game will always be keeping it between the bits of grass.'

Through no fault of his own, Peter Revson could not do that one fateful day at Kyalami, and like too many great drivers before him he paid the penalty for running out of luck. . .

Mark Donohue

Donohue, the epitome of the crew-cut all-American college boy to European eyes, achieved immense popularity with his easy manner, very pleasant personality and superb driving ability during the 1960s, and really reached full maturity with Roger Penske's team in the 1970s.

Born on March 18, 1937, in Summit, New Jersey, Donohue graduated from Brown University in 1959 with a BSc degree in mechanical engineering. He began racing that year, first with a private Chevrolet Corvette in which he won a hill-climb at his first attempt. By 1961 he was racing an Elva Courier in 'E Production' races, and after a season's battle with Revson's Morgan he won the class Championship.

In these early years he combined an engineering career with his own race preparation programme, and in 1965 he took two national championships, one in a 'B Production' Mustang and the other with a Formula C single-seater Lotus 20B.

The team — Roger Penske (left), entrant, and Mark Donohue (right), engineer-driver

It was veteran SCCA road racer Walt Hansgen who introduced the smooth, fast and intelligent Donohue to professional race driving, in 1966. Mark co-drove John Mecom's Ferrari with Hansgen early in the year, and then took a place in the Ford long-distance team, with Hansgen's backing.

In April, the veteran Hansgen died after crashing his Ford GT in the Le Mans test weekend, and Donohue joined forces with successful former amateur driver-turned-super successful motor trader, Roger Penske. The elegant Philadelphian entered beautifully-prepared Group 7 Lola-Chevrolets backed by the Sunoco oil company, and Donohue engineered and drove them to win the 1967 and 1968 US Road Racing Championships, and was runner-up in the inaugural CanAm Championship of 1966.

Donohue rapidly established himself as Champion of America's cause in CanAm racing, and in 1968 he won 10 out of 13 TransAm Championship touring car races to take the title in a Penske Chevrolet Camaro. He was voted 'Driver of the Year' by SCCA, an accolade he had also received back in 1965 in his days as a privateer with the Mustang and Lotus 20. . .

In 1969 'Captain Nice' retained his TransAm title for the Penske team, and co-drove with Chuck Parsons to bring a very battered Lola-Chevrolet coupe home to a lucky win in the Daytona 24-Hour race.

By this time Penske had turned his attention to track racing, and on his debut at Indianapolis with a typical impeccably-prepared four-wheel drive Lola-Offy, Donohue qualified fourth fastest in the field and ran third in the race until an 11-minute pit-stop to correct an ignition problem dropped him to seventh, where he finished. For this performance, he was voted 'Rookie of the Year'. Nearest challenger for the title that year was his old sparring partner, Peter Revson. . .

Penske Racing had abandoned CanAm sports car racing for their USAC involvement, and in the 1970 Indy 500 Donohue brought his Sunoco Lola home into second place, on the same lap at the finish as winner, Al Unser. The new Penske tie with American Motors produced a series of superbly engineered TransAm Javelins, and Donohue took them to several wins in this national Championship.

Penske's main programme in 1971 saw Donohue driving a Sunoco McLaren-Offy in USAC events. He qualified second quickest to Revson's similar works car at Indianapolis, and led the race until the car's transmission failed. He won the Schaeffer 500 at Pocono and a 200-miler at Michigan to show that Penske and Donohue posed a real threat to the establishment, and right at the end of the season he made his Formula 1 debut in a McLaren M19 hired from the works. First race was the wet, misty Canadian Grand Prix at Mosport, and he soldiered quietly into third place to score four World Championship points.

In 1972 Donohue was back at Indy with a McLaren and he won the 500-Mile classic in terrific style. Then came

Mark Donohue was an immensely impressive — and popular — early leader at Indy in 1971, running away from the field before his Penske-McLaren M16 failed him, and was later totalled by another car crashing into its parking lot. The following year nothing failed, and America's 'Captain Nice' won the '500'

When he attacked Formula 1 seriously in 1975 Donohue was late in realising just how savagely his opponents mal-treated their cars, throwing them into corners while he would be balancing his into the turns USAC-style. Here he is seen first time out in the Penske March 751, at Silverstone — the car in which he crashed after a tyre failure in Austria. . .

Penske's return to CanAm racing with a turbocharged Porsche 917, and Donohue gave notice that McLaren's six-year domination of the Championship was about to end when he blew everybody off at Mosport, only to be delayed by minor impeller problems. Then while testing at Road Atlanta the Porsche crashed mightily after a body panel tore free, and Mark was lucky to escape with nothing worse than damaged leg tendons.

George Follmer took over a second Porsche to clinch the CanAm title, but Donohue was back in a sister car for the last three rounds, and won on his return at Edmonton. The season had also seen him racing a Penske Matador in NASCAR events, but even their slick and painstaking operation proved too thinly spread to bring success.

In the new year, Donohue's latest Sunoco-Porsche dominated six of the eight CanAm rounds, and set new qualifying and race records in those he did not win. His underpowered Formula 5000 Lola-AMC was handled with typical cool skill in the L & M Championship, but Penske's USAC Eagle proved a failure.

With the CanAm Championship under his belt, and growing domestic problems, Donohue announced his retirement from racing at the end of the 1973 season. He intended to remain with Penske Racing as a project engineer and gifted test driver, for this was where their magnificent preparation and development skills were based.

Penske' enthusiasm for a Formula 1 programme changed all that, and in Canada in September Donohue re-appeared at the wheel of a brand-new Penske-Cosworth Grand Prix car.

Donohue's come-back showings with the new Penske were over-shadowed by the other American F1 debutante — the Vel's Parnelli car driven by Mario Andretti. After his lay-off Mark was over-weight and his reflexes seemed to have lost their conditioning. During 1975 the Penske car seemed to 'develop backwards' after an initial seventh place in Buenos Aires. Then, on the unusual Anderstorp circuit Mark finished fifth to score his first World Championship points in the car, and soon afterwards back-to-back testing between the Penske and a new March at Silverstone convinced the team to buy outside. In this car Mark was fifth at the rain-affected British GP (although he was one of those who crashed). A month later on August 17, the Penske March had a front tyre deflate in the super-fast right-hander after the pits at Oster-reichring. The car tore down several catch fences which bundled beneath the car and launched it into the air. Clearing an Armco barrier it fatally injured two helpless marshals then slammed into scaffolds supporting an advertising hoarding. Mark Donohue was taken from the car apparently only mildly concussed after one scaffold pole had struck his helmet. Tragically his condition rapidly deteriorated, and two days later he succumbed to a massive brain haemorrhage in Graz hospital. American and International motor racing had lost one of its most gifted and pleasant characters.

The Champions'Victories

Giuseppe Farina

1934	Masarykring Voiturette race, Brno	Maserati
1937	Naples GP	Alfa Romeo
1939	Antwerp GP sports car race	Alfa Romeo
	Coppa Ciano	Alfa Romeo
	Prix de Berne	Alfa Romeo
1940	Tripoli GP	Alfa Romeo
1946	GP des Nations, Geneva	Alfa Romeo
1948	GP des Nations, Geneva	Maserati
	Monaco GP	Maserati
	Mar del Plata GP	Maserati
	Circuito del Garda	Ferrari
1949	Rosario GP	Ferrari
	Lausanne GP	Maserati
1950	British GP	Alfa Romeo
	Swiss GP	Alfa Romeo
	Bari GP	Alfa Romeo
	BRDC International Trophy, Silverstone	Alfa Romeo
	Italian GP	Alfa Romeo

World Champion Driver

1951	International Trophy (Heat 2)	Alfa Romeo
	Paris GP, Bois de Boulogne	Maserati
	Ulster Trophy	Alfa Romeo
	Belgian GP	Alfa Romeo
	Goodwood Trophy	Alfa Romeo
	Woodcote Cup, Goodwood	Alfa Romeo
1952	Naples GP	Ferrari
	Monza Autodrome GP	Ferrari
1953	Rouen F1 GP	Ferrari
	Naples GP	Ferrari
	German GP	Ferrari
	Buenos Aires GP	Ferrari
	Daily Express Trophy Libre race, Silverstone	Thin Wall Special
	Spa 24 Hours (with Hawthorn)	Ferrari
	Nürburgring 1000Km (with Ascari)	Ferrari
	Casablanca 12 Hours	Ferrari
1954	Syracuse GP	Ferrari
	Argentine 1000Km (with Maglioli)	Ferrari
	Agadir sports car race	Ferrari

Juan Manuel Fangio

1940	International GP of the North	Chevrolet
1941	Getulio Vargas GP	Chevrolet
	Argentine 1000 Miles	Chevrolet
1942	Rosario GP	Chevrolet
	Mar y Sierra GP	Chevrolet
	Mar del Plata GP	Chevrolet
	Prix Doble Vuelta	Chevrolet
1947	E. Brosutti sports car race	Chevrolet special
	Springtime GP	Chevrolet
	Prix Doble Vuelta	Chevrolet
1948	Vuelta de Pringles GP	Chevrolet
	Otono GP	Chevrolet Special
	Vuelta de Entre Rios	Chevrolet
1949	Dona Eva Peron Meccanica Nacional	Chevrolet Special
	Mar del Plata GP	Maserati
	Fraile-Muerto-Belville GP	Chevrolet
	San Remo GP	Maserati
	Pau GP	Maserati
	GP du Rousillon, Perpignan	Maserati
	Marseilles GP	Simca-Gordini
	Autodrome GP, Monza	Ferrari
	Albi GP	Maserati
1950	Pau GP	Maserati
	San Remo GP	Alfa Romeo
	Monaco GP	Alfa Romeo
	Circuit des Ramparts, Angouleme	Maserati
	Belgian GP	Alfa Romeo
	French GP	Alfa Romeo
	GP des Nations, Geneva	Alfa Romeo
	Pescara GP	Alfa Romeo
	BRDC International Trophy (Heat 1)	Alfa Romeo
	GP Parana	Ferrari
	Santiago GP	Ferrari
	Argentine 500 Miles	Lago-Talbot
1951	BRDC International Trophy (Heat 1)	Alfa Romeo
	Swiss GP	Alfa Romeo
	French GP (with Fagioli)	Alfa Romeo
	Bari GP	Alfa Romeo
	Spanish GP	Alfa Romeo

World Champion Driver

1952	Interlagos GP, Sao Paulo	Ferrari
	Rio de Janeiro GP, Boa Vista	Ferrari
	Buenos Aires GP	Ferrari
	Argentine GP	Ferrari
	Piriapolis GP, Montevideo	Ferrari
	Uruguayan GP	Ferrari
1953	Albi GP (Heat 1)	BRM V16
	Supercortemaggiore sports car GP	Alfa Romeo
	Italian GP	Maserati
	Modena GP	Maserati
	Carrera Panamericana road race	Lancia
1954	Argentine GP	Maserati
	Belgian GP	Maserati
	French GP	Maserati
	German GP	Mercedes-Benz
	Swiss GP	Mercedes-Benz
	Italian GP	Mercedes-Benz

World Champion Driver

1955	Argentine GP	Mercedes-Benz
	Buenos Aires GP	Mercedes-Benz

Eifelrennen	Mercedes-Benz
Belgian GP	Mercedes-Benz
Dutch GP	Mercedes-Benz
Swedish sports car GP	Mercedes-Benz
Italian GP	Mercedes-Benz
Venezuelan sports car GP	Maserati

World Champion Driver

1956 Argentine GP (*with Musso*)	Ferrari
Mendoza GP	Ferrari
Sebring 12 Hours (*with Castellotti*)	Ferrari
Syracuse GP	Ferrari
British GP	Ferrari
German GP	Ferrari

World Champion Driver

1957 Argentine GP	Maserati
Buenos Aires GP	Maserati
Cuban sports car GP	Maserati
Sebring 12 Hours (*with Behra*)	Maserati
Monaco GP	Maserati
Portuguese sports car GP	Maserati
French GP	Maserati
German GP	Maserati
Interlagos sports car GP	Maserati
Rio de Janeiro sports car GP	Maserati

World Champion Driver

| 1958 Buenos Aires GP | Maserati |

Retired after placing 4th in French GP, July 9, 1958, driving a works Maserati 250F.

Alberto Ascari

1947 Modena sports car GP	Maserati
1948 San Remo GP	Maserati
1949 BRDC International Trophy	Ferrari
Italian GP	Ferrari
Swiss GP	Ferrari
Bari GP	Ferrari
Peron GP, Buenos Aires	Maserati
Coupe des Petites Cylindrées, Reims	Ferrari
1950 Modena GP (F2)	Ferrari
Mons GP (F2)	Ferrari
Luxembourg GP (F2)	Ferrari
Rome GP (F2), Caracalla Baths	Ferrari
Coupe des Petites Cylindrées	Ferrari
German GP (F2)	Ferrari
Circuito del Garda (F2)	Ferrari
Silverstone 1 Hour production race	Ferrari
Penya Rhin GP, Barcelona	Ferrari
1951 Monza Autodrome GP (F2)	Ferrari
Naples GP (F2)	Ferrari
Modena GP (F2)	Ferrari
San Remo GP	Ferrari

German GP	Ferrari
Italian GP	Ferrari
1952 Syracuse GP	Ferrari
Pau GP	Ferrari
Marseilles GP	Ferrari
Belgian GP	Ferrari
French GP	Ferrari
British GP	Ferrari
German GP	Ferrari
Comminges GP (*with Simon*)	Ferrari
Dutch GP	Ferrari
La Baule GP	Ferrari
Italian GP	Ferrari

World Champion Driver

1953 Argentine GP	Ferrari
Pau GP	Ferrari
Bordeaux GP	Ferrari
Dutch GP	Ferrari
Belgian GP	Ferrari
British GP	Ferrari
Swiss GP	Ferrari
Nürburgring 1000Km (*with Farina*)	Ferrari

World Champion Driver

1954 Mille Miglia	Lancia
1955 Naples GP	Lancia
Turin GP, Valentino Park	Lancia

Last race, 1955 Monaco GP, killed in Ferrari, Monza, 1955.

Mike Hawthorn

1951 Ulster Trophy Handicap	Riley
Leinster Trophy, Wicklow	Riley
1952 Chichester Cup, Goodwood	Cooper-Bristol
Lavant Cup, Goodwood	Cooper-Bristol
Sussex Trophy, Goodwood	Cooper-Bristol
Daily Mail Trophy, Boreham (F2)	Cooper-Bristol
Turnberry (F2)	Cooper-Bristol
Ibsley Formule Libre	Cooper-Bristol
1953 International Trophy, Silverstone	Ferrari
Ulster Trophy	Ferrari
French GP	Ferrari
Woodcote Cup, Goodwood	Thin Wall Special
Goodwood Trophy	Thin Wall Special
Daily Express production sports cars race, Silverstone	Ferrari
Spa 24 Hours (*with Farina*)	Ferrari
Pescara 12 Hours (*with Maglioli*)	Ferrari
1954 Spanish GP	Ferrari
Supercortemaggiore GP, Monza (*with Maglioli*)	Ferrari
1955 Le Mans 24 Hours (*with Bueb*)	Jaguar
Sebring 12 Hours (*with Walters*)	Jaguar
International Trophy, Crystal Palace	Maserati

1956 Supercortemaggiore GP (*with Collins*) — Ferrari
1958 Glover Trophy, Goodwood — Ferrari
French GP — Ferrari
Last race, 1958 Moroccan GP, retired at close of season.
World Champion Driver

Jack Brabham

1948/49 New South Wales, Australian & South Australian Midget Champion
1950/51 South Australian Champion
1952 Redex Champion of Australia — Cooper Mark IV
1953 Queensland & New South Wales Champion — Cooper-Bristol
1955 Australian GP — Cooper-Bristol (mid-engined)

1957 Brands Hatch (F2) — Cooper-Climax
Crystal Palace (F2) — Cooper-Climax
Prix de Paris (F2) — Cooper-Climax
Brands Hatch — Cooper-Climax
French GP (F2 class) (*with Mike MacDowell*) — Cooper-Climax
Rochester Trophy (F2) — Cooper-Climax
Oulton Park Gold Cup (F2) — Cooper-Climax
1958 Lavant Cup (F2) — Cooper-Climax
Casablanca GP (F2) — Cooper-Climax
Nürburgring 1000Km (*with Moss*) — Aston Martin
1959 Monaco GP — Cooper-Climax
British GP — Cooper-Climax
International Trophy Silverstone — Cooper-Climax
Lavant Cup (F2) — Cooper-Climax
Kentish 100 (F2) — Cooper-Climax
World Champion Driver
1960 Dutch GP — Cooper-Climax
Belgian GP — Cooper-Climax
French GP — Cooper-Climax
British GP — Cooper-Climax
Portuguese GP — Cooper-Climax
New Zealand GP — Cooper-Climax
Silver City Trophy (F1) — Cooper-Climax
Lady Wigram Trophy — Cooper-Climax
Bathurst — Cooper-Climax
Brussels GP (F2) — Cooper-Climax
Pau GP (F2) — Cooper-Climax
Roskilde (F2) — Cooper-Climax
World Champion Driver
1961 Brussels GP (F1) — Cooper-Climax
Aintree 200 (F1) — Cooper-Climax
Lombank Trophy Inter-Continental — Cooper-Climax
Guards Trophy Inter-Continental — Cooper-Climax
New Zealand GP — Cooper-Climax
Lady Wigram Trophy — Cooper-Climax

Riverside sports cars — Cooper Monaco
1962 Copenhagen GP (F1) — Lotus 24
Vic Hudson Trophy Levin — Cooper-Climax
Lakeside — Cooper-Climax
Sandown Park — Cooper-Climax
1963 Solitude GP — Brabham
Austrian GP — Brabham
Hudson Trophy Levin — Brabham
Australian GP — Brabham
1964 Aintree 200 — Brabham
Australian GP — Brabham
Warwick Farm 100 — Brabham
Lakeside — Brabham
Karlskoga (F2) — Brabham
Albi GP (F2) — Brabham
Oulton Park Gold Cup (F2) — Brabham
Ile de France (F2) — Brabham
Snetterton saloons — Ford Galaxie
1965 Karlskoga (F2) — Brabham
Sandown Park — Brabham
Rand GP — Brabham
1966 French GP — Brabham
British GP — Brabham
German GP — Brabham
Dutch GP — Brabham
International Trophy Silverstone — Brabham
Oulton Park Gold Cup — Brabham
Sunday Mirror (F2) — Brabham-Honda
Pau GP (F2) — Brabham-Honda
Barcelona (F2) — Brabham-Honda
Zolder (F2) — Brabham-Honda
Crystal Palace (F2) — Brabham-Honda
Reims (F2) — Brabham-Honda
Karlskoga (F2) — Brabham-Honda
Keimola (F2) — Brabham-Honda
Ile de France (F2) — Brabham-Honda
Albi GP (F2) — Brabham-Honda
Snetterton saloons — Ford Galaxie
World Champion Driver
1967 French GP — Brabham
Canadian GP — Brabham
Oulton Park Spring Cup (F1) — Brabham
Oulton Park Gold Cup (F1) — Brabham
Longford Tasmania — Brabham
1969 International Trophy Silverstone — Brabham
1970 South African GP — Brabham
Paris 1000Km (*with Francois Cevert*) — Matra-Simca

Phil Hill

Year	Event	Car
1948	Carrell Speedway	MG TC
1950	Pebble Beach	Jaguar XK120
1955	Nassau Trophy	Ferrari 3·5
1956	Swedish GP sports cars (*with Maurice Trintignant*)	Ferrari
	Messina 5 Hours	Ferrari
1957	Caracas 1000Km (*with Peter Collins*)	Ferrari 4·1
1958	Argentine 1000Km (*with Collins*)	Ferrari
	Sebring 12 Hours (*with Collins*)	Ferrari
	Le Mans 24 Hours (*with Olivier Gendebien*)	Ferrari
1959	Riverside sports cars	Ferrari
1960	Italian GP	Ferrari
	Argentine 1000Km (*with Cliff Allison*)	Ferrari
1961	Belgian GP	Ferrari
	Italian GP	Ferrari
	Sebring 12 Hours (*with Gendebien*)	Ferrari
	Le Mans 24 Hours (*with Gendebien*)	Ferrari
	World Champion Driver	
1962	Nürburgring 1000Km (*with Gendebien*)	Ferrari V6
	Le Mans 24 Hours (*with Gendebien*)	Ferrari V12
1964	Daytona 2000Km (*with Pedro Rodriguez*)	Ferrari GTO
1966	Nürburgring 1000Km (*with Jo Bonnier*)	Chaparral 2D
	Monterey GP CanAm	Chaparral 2E
1967	BOAC 500 Brands Hatch (*with Mike Spence*)	Chaparral 2F

Graham Hill

Year	Event	Car
1957	British Empire Trophy	Lotus 15
1959	Mallory Park sports	Lotus 17
	Brands Hatch sports	Lotus 17
1961	Oulton Park GT	Jaguar E-Type
1962	Dutch GP	BRM
	German GP	BRM
	Italian GP	BRM
	Glover Trophy F1	BRM
	International Trophy Silverstone	BRM
	Scott-Brown Trophy	Lotus 19
	World Champion Driver	
1963	Monaco GP	BRM
	United States GP	BRM
	Lombank Trophy F1	BRM
	Aintree 200	BRM
	Lombank Trophy GT	Jaguar E-Type
	Sussex Trophy GT	Jaguar E-Type
	BRDC GT race	Jaguar E-Type
	Grovewood Trophy GT	Jaguar E-Type
	RAC Tourist Trophy	Ferrari 250GTO

Year	Event	Car
	St Mary's Trophy	Jaguar 3·8
	Aintree saloons	Jaguar 3·8
1964	Monaco GP	BRM
	United States GP	BRM
	Snetterton (F2)	Brabham
	New Zealand GP	Brabham
	Rheims 12 Hours (*with Jo Bonnier*)	Ferrari
	RAC Tourist Trophy	Ferrari
	Paris 1000Km (*with Jo Bonnier*)	Ferrari
	Rand GP	Brabham
	Sussex Trophy	Ferrari
	BRDC Silverstone	Ferrari
1965	New Zealand GP	Brabham
	Snetterton (F2)	Brabham
	Monaco GP	BRM
	United States GP	BRM
1966	New Zealand GP	BRM
	Australian GP	BRM
	Indianapolis 500	Lola
1968	Spanish GP	Lotus 49
	Monaco GP	Lotus 49B
	Mexican GP	Lotus 49B
	World Champion Driver	
1969	Monaco GP	Lotus 49B
	Albi GP (F2)	Lotus 59
1971	International Trophy Silverstone	Brabham
	Thruxton (F2)	Brabham
1972	Monza Lottery GP (F2)	Brabham
	Le Mans 24 Hours (*with Pescarolo*)	Matra-Simca

Jim Clark

Year	Event	Car
1956	Stobs Camp Sprint	Sunbeam Mk 3
	Winfield Sprint	DKW *Sonderklasse* & Sunbeam (2 class wins each)
1957	BMRC Charterhall	Porsche 1600S
	Winfield Sprint	Porsche 1600S
1958	Full Sutton	Jaguar D-Type (2 wins)
	Winfield Sprint	Porsche
	Full Sutton	Jaguar D-Type (2 wins)
		Porsche 1600S
	Stobs Camp Sprint	Porsche
	Crimond	Jaguar D-Type
	Rest-and-be-Thankful hillclimb	Porsche 1600S
	Charterhall	Jaguar D-Type (2 wins)
	Rest-and-be-Thankful	Porsche 1600S
	Charterhall	Jaguar D-Type
	Full Sutton	Jaguar D-Type (2 wins)
		Porsche

Winfield Sprint	Porsche (2 class wins)	Belgian GP	Lotus 25
	Jaguar D-Type	Dutch GP	Lotus 25
		French GP	Lotus 25
Mallory Park	Jaguar D-Type	British GP	Lotus 25
1959 Mallory Park	Lister-Jaguar (3 wins)	Brands Hatch	Ford Galaxie
		Swedish GP*	Lotus 25
	Lotus Elite	Milwaukee 200	Lotus 29
Charterhall	Lister-Jaguar (2 wins)	Italian GP	Lotus 25
		Oulton Park Gold Cup	Lotus 25
Rufforth	Lister-Jaguar	Oulton Park sports cars	Lotus 23
Stobs Camp Sprint	Porsche 1600S (2 class wins)	Snetterton 3 Hours	Lotus 23
		Snetterton saloon car race	Lotus-Cortina
		Riverside GP	Lotus 23
Bo'ness Hillclimb	Lister-Jaguar	Mexican GP	Lotus 25
	Lotus Elite	South African GP	Lotus 25
Winfield Sprint	Lister-Jaguar (2 class wins & FTD)	**World Champion Driver**	
		1964 Snetterton saloon cars	Lotus-Cortina (class win)
	Lotus Elite	Sebring saloon cars	Lotus-Cortina (class win)
Brands Hatch World Cup	Lotus Elite	Goodwood International Trophy	Lotus 25
	Lister-Jaguar	Goodwood saloon cars	Lotus-Cortina (class win)
Mallory Park	Lister-Jaguar		
	Lotus Elite	Pau GP (F2)	Lotus 32
Oulton Park	Lotus Elite	Oulton Park saloons	Lotus-Cortina
Charterhall	Lotus Elite	Oulton Park GT race	Lotus Elan
Charterhall	Lister-Jaguar (2 wins)	Oulton Park sports cars	Lotus 19
		Eifelrennen (F2)	Lotus 32
Snetterton 3 Hours	Lotus Elite	Silverstone saloon cars	Lotus-Cortina (class win)
1960 Goodwood FJ	Lotus 18		
Oulton Park FJ	Lotus 18	Silverstone GT race	Lotus Elan (class win)
Goodwood FJ	Lotus 18		
Silverstone FJ	Lotus 18	Grovewood Trophy (F2)	Lotus 32
Solitude FJ	Lotus 18	Mallory Guards Trophy	Lotus 30
Brands Hatch FJ	Lotus 18	Crystal Palace saloons	Lotus-Cortina
Kentish 100 (F2)	Lotus 18	Dutch GP	Lotus 25
Snetterton FJ	Lotus 18	Belgian GP	Lotus 25
Oulton Park FJ	Lotus 18 (2 wins)	British GP	Lotus 25
		Solitude GP	Lotus 25
Brands Hatch FJ	Lotus 18	British Eagle Trophy (F2)	Lotus 32
1961 Pau GP	Lotus 18 F1	Brands Hatch saloons	Lotus-Cortina (class win)
Rand GP	Lotus 21		
Natal GP	Lotus 21	Oulton Park saloons	Lotus-Cortina
South African GP*	Lotus 21	1965 South African GP	Lotus 33
*Non-Championship race		New Zealand GP heat	Lotus 32B
1962 Lombank Trophy (F1)	Lotus 24	Levin heat	Lotus 32B
Aintree 200 (F1)	Lotus 24	Levin Final	Lotus 32B
Belgian GP	Lotus 25	Levin 'Farewell' race	Lotus 32B
British GP	Lotus 25	Lady Wigram Trophy heat	Lotus 32B
Oulton Park Gold Cup	Lotus 25	Lady Wigram Trophy Final	Lotus 32B
Snetterton 3 Hours	Lotus 23	Teretonga Trophy heat	Lotus 32B
United States GP	Lotus 25	Teretonga Trophy Final	Lotus 32B
Mexican GP*	Lotus 25	Warwick Farm 100	Lotus 32B
Rand GP	Lotus 25	Lakeside Trophy	Lotus 32B
*Non-Championship race		Race of Champions heat	Lotus 33
1963 British Empire Trophy	Lotus 23	Silverstone Guards Trophy	Lotus 30
Pau GP	Lotus 25	Sebring 3 Hours	Lotus-Cortina
Imola GP	Lotus 25	Syracuse GP	Lotus 33
Silverstone International Trophy	Lotus 25	Goodwood International Trophy	Lotus 33
Crystal Palace	Lotus 23	Goodwood sports cars	Lotus 30

Year	Race	Car
	Goodwood saloon cars	Lotus-Cortina
	Pau GP (F2)	Lotus 32
	Indianapolis 500	Lotus 38
	Crystal Palace (F2)	Lotus 35 (2 heats and final)
	Belgian GP	Lotus 33
	French GP	Lotus 25
	Reims GP (F2)	Lotus 35
	British GP	Lotus 33
	German GP	Lotus 33
	British Eagle Trophy (F2)	Lotus 35
	World Champion Driver	
1966	Warwick Farm 100	Lotus 39
	Snetterton saloons	Lotus-Cortina (class win)
	Guards Trophy Brands heat	Felday 4
	Guards saloons	Lotus-Cortina
	Oulton Park saloons	Lotus-Cortina
	United States GP	Lotus 43
1967	Levin	Lotus 33
	Lady Wigram Trophy	Lotus 33
	Teretonga Trophy	Lotus 33
	Lakeside Trophy	Lotus 33
	Sandown Park	Lotus 33
	Barcelona (F2)	Lotus 48
	Zolder (F2 heat)	Lotus 48
	Dutch GP	Lotus 49
	British GP	Lotus 49
	Jarama (F2)	Lotus 48
	Keimola (F2)	Lotus 48
	United States GP	Lotus 49
	Mexican GP	Lotus 49
	Spanish GP*	Lotus 49
	*Non-Championship race	
1968	South African GP	Lotus 49
	Lady Wigram Trophy	Lotus 49T
	Surfers Paradise	Lotus 49T
	Warwick Farm	Lotus 49T
	Australian GP	Lotus 49T

John Surtees

Year	Race	Car
953	27 wins in 40 motor-cycle races	
1954	40 wins in 55 motor-cycle races	
1955	68 wins in 76 motor-cycle races	
1956	500cc motor-cycle World Champion	MV Agusta
1958 /59 /60	350cc and 500cc motor-cycle World Champion	
1961	Lombank Trophy (F1)	Cooper-Climax
	Glover Trophy (F1)	Cooper-Climax
1962	Mallory Park 2000Gns (F1)	Lola
	Longford Tasmania	Cooper-Climax
1963	German GP	Ferrari
	Mediterranean GP	Ferrari
	Rand GP	Ferrari
	Sebring 12 Hours (*with Ludovico Scarfiotti*)	Ferrari 250P
	Nürburgring 1000Km (*with Willy Mairesse*)	Ferrari 250P
	Lakeside	Lola
1964	German GP	Ferrari
	Italian GP	Ferrari
	Syracuse	Ferrari
	World Champion Driver	
1965	Oulton Park Gold Cup (F2)	Lola
	Nürburgring 1000Km (*with Scarfiotti*)	Ferrari 330P2
	Players 200 Mosport	Lola
1966	Belgian GP	Ferrari
	Mexican GP	Ferrari
	Monza 1000Km (*with Mike Parkes*)	Ferrari 330P3
	Guards Trophy Brands Hatch	Lola
	Times GP CanAm	Lola
	Stardust GP CanAm	Lola
1967	Italian GP	Honda
	Guards Mallory Park (F2)	Lola
	Zolder (F2)	Lola
	Stardust GP CanAm	Lola
1970	Oulton Park Gold Cup (F1)	Surtees
1971	Oulton Park Gold Cup (F1)	Surtees
1972	Imola (F2)	Surtees
	Japanese GP	Surtees

Denny Hulme

Year	Race	Car
1960	NZIGPA Driver to Europe Scholarship	
	Pescara FJ	Cooper-BMC
1961	Dunedin	Cooper-Climax
1963	Aintree FJ	Brabham
	Crystal Palace FJ	Brabham
1964	Hudson Trophy Levin	Brabham
	Clermont (F2)	Brabham
1965	Oulton Park (F2)	Brabham
	RAC Tourist Trophy	Brabham
1966	Rouen (F2)	Brabham-Honda
	Bugatti (F2)	Brabham-Honda
	Scott-Brown Trophy	Lola
	RAC Tourist Trophy	Lola
	Silverstone sports cars	Lola
1967	Monaco GP	Brabham
	German GP	Brabham
	Silverstone sports	Ford GT40
	World Champion Driver	
1968	Italian GP	McLaren
	Canadian GP	McLaren
	Silverstone International Trophy	McLaren
	Players Trophy Silverstone	Lola
	RAC Tourist Trophy	Lola
	Martini Trophy	Lola
	Elkhart Lake CanAm	McLaren
	Edmonton CanAm	McLaren
	Stardust GP CanAm	McLaren

1969 Mexican GP	McLaren
Silverstone sports	Lola
Edmonton CanAm	McLaren
Lexington CanAm	McLaren
Bridgehampton CanAm	McLaren
Riverside CanAm	McLaren
1970 Watkins Glen CanAm	McLaren
Edmonton CanAm	McLaren
Mid-Ohio CanAm	McLaren
Donnybrooke CanAm	McLaren
Laguna Seca CanAm	McLaren
Riverside CanAm	McLaren
1971 Mosport CanAm	McLaren
Edmonton CanAm	McLaren
Riverside CanAm	McLaren
1972 South African GP	McLaren
Oulton Park Gold Cup	McLaren
Mosport CanAm	McLaren
Watkins Glen CanAm	McLaren
1973 Swedish GP	McLaren
1974 Argentine GP	McLaren

Jackie Stewart

1963 14 victories in British club racing with Ecurie Ecosse Tojeiro-Buicks and Cooper Monaco — most successful club driver of the year.	
1964 Snetterton (F3)	Cooper-BMC
Goodwood (F3)	Cooper-BMC
Oulton Park (F3)	Cooper-BMC
Aintree (F3)	Cooper-BMC
Silverstone (F3)	Cooper-BMC
Monaco (F3)	Cooper-BMC
Mallory Park (F3)	Cooper-BMC
Rouen (F3)	Cooper-BMC
Reims (F3)	Cooper-BMC
Zandvoort (F3)	Cooper-BMC
Oulton Park (F3)	Cooper-BMC
Zolder GP (F2 heat)	Lotus 32
Vanwall Trophy (F2)	Lotus 32
Rand GP (F1 heat)	Lotus 33
1965 International Trophy Silverstone	BRM
Italian GP	BRM
1966 Monaco GP	BRM
Surfers Paradise 12 Hours (with Andy Buchanan)	Ferrari 275LM
Lady Wigram Trophy	BRM
Teretonga Trophy	BRM
Sandown Park	BRM
Longford	BRM
Tasman Champion	
Mount Fuji USAC race	Lola
1967 Oulton Park Gold Cup (F2)	Matra
Albi GP (F2)	Matra
1968 Dutch GP	Matra
German GP	Matra
United States GP	Matra
Oulton Park Gold Cup (F1)	Matra
Barcelona (F2)	Matra
Pau GP (F2)	Matra

Reims (F2)	Matra
1969 South African GP	Matra
Spanish GP	Matra
Dutch GP	Matra
French GP	Matra
British GP	Matra
Italian GP	Matra
Race of Champions	Matra
Eifelrennen (F2)	Matra
Jarama (F2)	Matra
World Champion Driver	
1970 Race of Champions	March
Spanish GP	March
Crystal Palace (F2)	Brabham
1971 Spanish GP	Tyrrell
Monaco GP	Tyrrell
French GP	Tyrrell
British GP	Tyrrell
German GP	Tyrrell
Canadian GP	Tyrrell
Ste Jovite CanAm	Lola
Lexington CanAm	Lola
World Champion Driver	
1972 Argentine GP	Tyrrell
French GP	Tyrrell
Canadian GP	Tyrrell
United States GP	Tyrrell
1973 South African GP	Tyrrell
Belgian GP	Tyrrell
Monaco GP	Tyrrell
Dutch GP	Tyrrell
German GP	Tyrrell
World Champion Driver	

Jochen Rindt

1965 Reims (F2)	Brabham
Le Mans 24 Hours (with Masten Gregory)	Ferrari 275LM
Prix du Tyrol	Abarth 2000
1966 Eifelrennen (F2)	Brabham
Motor Show 200 (F2)	Brabham
Sebring 4 Hours	Alfa Romeo GTA
1967 Guards Trophy (F2)	Brabham
Wills Silverstone (F2)	Brabham
Pau GP (F2)	Brabham
Eifelrennen (F2)	Brabham
Reims (F2)	Brabham
Rouen (F2)	Brabham
Langenlebarn (F2)	Brabham
Guards Brands Hatch (F2)	Brabham
Hameenlinna (F2)	Brabham
1968 Thruxton (F2)	Brabham
Zolder (F2)	Brabham
Crystal Palace (F2)	Brabham
Rhine Cup (F2)	Brabham
Langenlebarn (F2)	Brabham
Enna (F2)	Brabham
1969 United States GP	Lotus 49B
Thruxton (F2)	Lotus 59B
Pau GP (F2)	Lotus 59B
Zolder (F2)	Lotus 59B

Langenlebarn (F2)	Lotus 59B
Lady Wigram Trophy	Lotus 49T
Warwick Farm 100	Lotus 49T
1970 Monaco GP	Lotus 49C
French GP	Lotus 72
Dutch GP	Lotus 72
British GP	Lotus 72
German GP	Lotus 72
Thruxton (F2)	Lotus 59B
Pau GP (F2)	Lotus 59B
Eifelrennen (F2)	Lotus 59B
Zolder (F2)	Lotus 59B

Posthumous World Champion Driver

Emerson Fittipaldi

1965 Sao Paulo Kart Champion & Group 2 Novices' Champion of Rio de Janeiro	
1967 Brazilian Formula Vee Champion	
1968 Interlagos 12 Hours (with Wilson Fittipaldi)	Volkswagen
1969 Lombank Formula 3 Champion	Lotus 59
1970 United States GP	Lotus 72
1971 Madrid GP (F2)	Lotus 69
Crystal Palace (F2)	Lotus 69
Albi GP (F2)	Lotus 69
Interlagos (F2)	Lotus 69
Interlagos (F2)	Lotus 69
1972 Spanish GP	Lotus 72
Belgian GP	Lotus 72
British GP	Lotus 72
Austrian GP	Lotus 72
Italian GP	Lotus 72
Race of Champions	Lotus 72
Rome GP	Lotus 72
Rothmans 50,000	Lotus 72
Rindt Trophy (F2)	Lotus 69
Rouen (F2)	Lotus 69
Osterreichring (F2)	Lotus 69
Interlagos (F2)	Lotus 69

World Champion Driver

1973 Argentine GP	Lotus 72
Brazilian GP	Lotus 72
Spanish GP	Lotus 72
1974 Brazilian GP	McLaren
Belgian GP	McLaren
Canadian GP	McLaren

World Champion Driver

| 1975 Argentine GP | McLaren |
| British GP | McLaren |

Niki Lauda

1970 Oulton Park (F2)	March
1973 Monza 4 Hours (with Brian Muir)	BMW
1974 Spanish GP	Ferrari
Dutch GP	Ferrari
1975 Monaco GP	Ferrari
Belgian GP	Ferrari
Swedish GP	Ferrari
French GP	Ferrari
United States GP	Ferrari

World Champion Driver

1976 Brazilian GP	Ferrari
South African GP	Ferrari
Belgian GP	Ferrari
Monaco GP	Ferrari
British GP*	Ferrari
1977 South African GP	Ferrari

*'Won' on the disqualification of James Hunt

James Hunt

1970 Rouen (F3)	Lotus 59
Zolder (F3)	Lotus 59
1971 Montlhery (F3)	March
Nürburgring (F3)	March
Crystal Palace (F3)	March
Brands Hatch (F3)	March
1974 Silverstone International Trophy	Hesketh
1975 Dutch GP	Hesketh
1976 Spanish GP*	McLaren
French GP	McLaren
British GP**	McLaren
German GP	McLaren
Dutch GP	McLaren
Canadian GP	McLaren
United States GP	McLaren

World Champion Driver

| 1977 Race of Champions | McLaren |

* Hunt's win with this illegal car subsequently confirmed by FIA after initial disqualification.
**Hunt's win subsequently declared null by FIA on Ferrari appeal hearing.

The World Championships

1950	Farina	30 points
	Fangio	27
	Fagioli	24
1951	Fangio	31
	Ascari	25
	Gonzales	24
1952	Ascari	36
	Farina	25
	Taruffi	22
1953	Ascari	34½
	Fangio	28
	Farina	26
1954	Fangio	42
	Gonzales	25
	Hawthorn	24
1955	Fangio	40
	Moss	23
	Casttelloti	12
1956	Fangio	30
	Moss	27
	Collins	25
1957	Fangio	40
	Moss	25
	Musso	16
1958	Hawthorn	42
	Moss	41
	Brooks	24

1959	Brabham	31 points
	Brooks	27
	Moss	25½
1960	Brabham	43
	McLaren	34
	Moss	19
1961	P. Hill	34
	von Trips	33
	Moss and	
	Gurney	21
1962	G. Hill	42
	Clark	30
	McLaren	27
1963	Clark	54
	G. Hill	29
	Ginther	29
1964	Surtees	40
	G. Hill	39
	Clark	32
1965	Clark	54
	G. Hill	40
	Stewart	33
1966	Brabham	42
	Surtees	28
	Rindt	22
1967	Hulme	51
	Brabham	46
	Clark	41

1968	G. Hill	48 points
	Stewart	36
	Hulme	33
1969	Stewart	63
	Ickx	37
	McLaren	26
1970	Rindt	45
	Ickx	40
	Regazzoni	33
1971	Stewart	62
	Peterson	33
	Cevert	26
1972	Fittipaldi	61
	Stewart	45
	Hulme	39
1973	Stewart	71
	Fittipaldi	55
	Peterson	52
1974	Fittipaldi	55
	Regazzoni	52
	Sheckter	45
1975	Lauda	64½
	Fittipaldi	45
	Reutemann	37
1976	Hunt	69
	Lauda	68
	Scheckter	49

156